When God Is a Customer

With deep sorrow we note the death of
our beloved friend and co-author, A. K. Ramanujan,
on July 13, 1993, when this book was
in press.

When God Is a Customer

Telugu Courtesan Songs by
Kṣetrayya and Others

Edited and Translated by
A. K. Ramanujan, Velcheru Narayana Rao,
and David Shulman

UNIVERSITY OF CALIFORNIA PRESS

Berkeley Los Angeles London

University of California Press
Berkeley and Los Angeles, California

University of California Press, Ltd.
London, England

Library of Congress Cataloging-in-Publication Data

When God is a customer : Telugu courtesan songs / by Kṣetrayya and others ; edited and translated by A. K. Ramanujan, Velcheru Narayana Rao, and David Dean Shulman.
p. cm.
Includes bibliographical references and index.
ISBN 0-520-08068-8 (alk. paper). — ISBN 0-520-08069-6 (pbk. : alk. paper)
1. Telugu poetry—Translations into English. 2. Telugu poetry—1500–1800—History and criticism. 3. Music—India—17th century—History and criticism. 4. Music—India—18th century—History and criticism. I. Kṣētrayya, 17th cent. II. Ramanujan, A. K., 1929– . III. Nārāyaṇarāvu, Vēlcēru, 1932– . IV. Shulman, David Dean, 1949– .
PL4780.65.E5W47 1994
894'.82713—dc20 93-28264
CIP

Printed in the United States of America
1 2 3 4 5 6 7 8 9

The paper used in this publication meets the minimum requirements of America National Standard for Information Sciences—Permanence of Paper for Printed Library Materials, ANSI Z39.48-1984. ♾

for Wendy Doniger

vijñānasāmastyamayāntareva
sākāratāsiddhimayākhileva

wholly graced with embodied passion,
with the fullness of wisdom within her

Naiṣadhīyacarita 10.88

Contents

Preface 1

Introduction 9

The Songs

ANNAMAYYA 43

RUDRAKAVI 55

KṢETRAYYA 61

SĀRAṄGAPĀṆI 129

Poem to Lord
KŌṄKAṆEŚVARA 143

Notes to the Text 149
Notes to the Songs 153
Index of Refrains 157

Preface

The poems translated here belong to the category of *padams*—short musical compositions of a light classical nature, intended to be sung and, often, danced. Originally, they belonged to the professional caste of dancers and singers, *devadāsīs* or *veśyās* (and their male counterparts, the *naṭṭuvaṉār* musicians), who were associated with both temples and royal courts in late medieval South India. *Padams* were composed throughout India, early examples in Sanskrit occurring in Jayadeva's famous devotional poem, the *Gītagovinda* (twelfth century).[1] In South India the genre assumed a standardized form in the second half of the fifteenth century with the Telugu *padams* composed by the great temple-poet Tāḷḷapāka Annamācārya, also known by the popular name Annamayya, at Tirupati.[2] This form includes an opening line called *pallavi* that functions as a refrain, often in conjunction with the second line, *anupallavi*. This refrain is repeated after each of the (usually three) *caraṇam* verses. *Padams* have been and are still being composed in the major languages of South India: Telugu, Tamil, and Kannada. However, the *padam* tradition reached its expressive peak in Telugu, the primary language for South Indian classical music, during the fifteenth to eighteenth centuries in southern Andhra and the Tamil region.[3]

In general, Telugu *padams* are devotional in character and thus find their place within the wider corpus of South Indian *bhakti* poetry. The early examples by Annamayya are wholly located within the context of temple worship and are directed toward the deity Veṅkaṭeśvara and his consort, Alamelumaṅga, at the Tirupati shrine. Later poets, such as Kṣetrayya, the central figure in this volume, seem to have composed their songs outside the temples, but they nevertheless usually mention the deity as the male protagonist of the poem. Indeed, the god's title—Muvva Gopāla for Kṣetrayya, Veṇugopāla for his successor Sāraṅgapāṇi—serves as an identifying "signature," a *mudrā*, for each of these poets. The god assumes here the role of a lover, seen, for the most part, through the eyes of one of his courtesans, mistresses, or wives, whose persona the poet adopts. These are, then, devotional works of an erotic cast, composed by male poets using a feminine voice and performed by women. As such, they articulate the relationship between the devotee and his god in terms of an intensely imagined erotic experience, expressed in bold but also delicately nuanced tones. Their devotional character notwithstanding, one can also read them as simple love poems. Indeed, one often feels that, for Kṣetrayya at least, the devotional component, with its suggestive ironies, is overshadowed by the emotional and sensual immediacy of the material.

The Three Major Poets of the Padam Tradition

Tāḷḷapāka Annamācārya (1424–1503), a Telugu Brahmin, represents to perfection the Telugu temple-poet.[4] Legend, filling out his image, claims he refused to sing before one of the Vijayanagara kings, Sāḷuva Narasimharāya, so exclusively was his devotion focused upon the god. Apparently supported by the temple establishment at Tirupati, located on the boundary between the Telugu and Tamil regions, Annamayya composed over fourteen thousand *padams* to the god Veṅkaṭeśvara. The poems were engraved on copperplates and kept in the temple, where they were rediscovered, hidden in a locked room, in the second decade of this century. Colophons on the copperplates divide Annamayya's poems into two major types—*śṛṅgārasaṅkīrtanalu*, those of an erotic nature, and *adhyātmasaṅkīrtanalu*, "metaphysical" poems. Annamayya's sons and grandsons continued to compose devotional works at Tirupati, creating a Tāḷḷapāka corpus of truly enormous scope. His grandson Cinatirumalācārya even wrote a *śāstra*-like normative grammar for *padam* poems, the *Saṅkīrtanalakṣaṇamu*.

We know next to nothing about the most versatile and central of the Telugu *padam* poets, Kṣetrayya (or Kṣetraya). His god is Muvva Gopāla, the Cowherd of Muvva (or, alternatively, Gopāla of the Jingling Bells), and he mentions a village called Muvvapuri in some of his poems. This has led scholars to locate his birthplace in the village of Muvva or Mŏvva, near Kūcipūḍi (the center of the Kūcipūḍi dance tradition), in Krishna district. There is a temple in this village to Krishna as the cowherd (*gopāla*). Still, the association of Kṣetrayya with Muvva is far from certain, and even if that village was indeed the poet's first home, he is most clearly associated with places far to the south, in Tamil Nadu of the Nāyaka period. A famous *padam* by this poet tells us he sang two thousand *padams* for King Tirumala Nāyaka of Madurai, a thousand for Vijayarāghava, the last Nāyaka king of Tañjāvūr, and fifteen hundred, composed in forty days, before the Padshah of Golconda.[5] This dates him securely to the mid-seventeenth century. Of these thousands of poems, less than four hundred survive. In addition to

Muvva Gopāla, the poet sometimes mentions other deities or human patrons (the two categories having merged in Nāyaka times).[6] Thus we have poems on the gods Ādivarāha, Kañci Varada, Cĕvvandi Liṅgaḍu, Tilla Govindarāja, Kaḍapa Veṅkaṭeśa, Hemādrisvāmi, Yadugiri Celuvarāyaḍu, Vedanārāyaṇa, Pālagiri Cĕnnuḍu, Tiruvallūri Vīrarāghava, Śrī Raṅgeśa, Madhurāpurīśa, Satyapuri Vāsudeva, and Śrī Nāgaśaila Mallikārjuna, as well as on the kings Vijayarāghava Nāyaka and Tupākula Veṅkaṭakṛṣṇa. The range of deities is sometimes used to explain this poet's name—Kṣetrayya or, in Sanskritized form, Kṣetrajña, "one who knows sacred places"—so that he becomes yet another peripatetic *bhakti* poet-saint, singing his way from temple to temple. But this explanation smacks of popular etymology and certainly distorts the poet's image. Despite the modern stories and improvised legends about him current today in South India, Kṣetrayya belongs less to the temple than to the courtesans' quarters of the Nāyaka royal towns. We see him as a poet composing for, and with the assumed persona of, the sophisticated and cultured courtesans who performed before gods and kings.[7] This community of highly literate performers, the natural consumers of Kṣetrayya's works, provides an entirely different cultural context than Annamayya's temple-setting. Kṣetrayya thus gives voice, in rather realistic vignettes taken from the ambience of the South Indian courtesans he knew, to a major shift in the development of the Telugu *padam*.

If Kṣetrayya perhaps marks the *padam* tradition at its most subtle and refined, Sāraṅgapāṇi, in the early eighteenth century, shows us its further evolution in the direction of a yet more concrete, imaginative, and sometimes coarse eroticism. He is linked with the little kingdom of Kārveṭinagaram in the Chittoor district of southern Andhra and with the minor ruler Mākarāju Veṅkaṭa Pĕrumāḷ Rāju (d. 1732). Only some two hundred *padams* by this poet survive in print, nearly all of them addressed to the god Veṇugopāla of Kārveṭinagaram. A few of the poems attributed to Sāraṅgapāṇi also appear in the Kṣetrayya collections, despite the palpable difference in tone between the two poets.

These names by no means exhaust the list of *padam* composers in Telugu. The Maratha kings of Tañjāvūr figure as the patron-lovers in a rich literature of *padams* composed at their court.[8] Similar works were sung in the palaces of zamindars throughout South India right up to modern times. With the abolition of the *devadāsī* tradition by the British, *padams,* like other genres proper to this community, made their way to the concert stage. They still comprise a major part of the repertoire of classical vocal music and dance, alongside related forms such as the *kīrttanam* (which is never danced).

A Note on the Translation

We have selected the poems that follow largely on the basis of our own tastes, from the large collections of *padams* by Annamayya, Kṣetrayya, and Sāraṅgapāṇi. We have also included a translation of Kandukūri Rudrakavi's *Janārdanāṣṭakamu,* a poem dating from the early sixteenth century and linked thematically (but not formally) with the emerging *padam* tradition. An anonymous *padam* addressed to Kŏṅkaṇésvara closes the translation. To some extent, we were also guided by a list prepared by T. Visvanathan, of Wesleyan University, of *padams* current in his own family tradition. Some of the poems included here are among the most popular in current performances in South India; others were chosen because they seemed to us representative of the poets, or simply because of their lyrical and expressive qualities.

In general, we have adhered closely to the literal force of the Telugu text and to the order of its sentences. At times, though, because of the colloquial and popular character of some of these texts, we have allowed ourselves to paraphrase slightly, using an English idiom or expression. We have also frequently removed, as tedious in translation, the repeated vocatives that dot the verses—as when the courtesan speaks to her friend, who is habitually referred to by conventional epithets such as *vanajākṣiro*, "woman with lotus-eyes," or *komaliro*, "delicate lady." Telugu is graced with a truly remarkable number of nouns meaning "woman," and these are amply represented in our texts. The heroine is sometimes referred to by stylized titles such as *kanakāṅgi*, "having a golden body," epithets that could also be interpreted as proper names. For the most part, this wealth of feminine reference, so beautifully evocative in the original, finds only pale and reductive equivalents in the English.

The format we have adopted seeks to mirror the essential features of the original, above all the division into stanzas and the role of the *pallavi* refrain. While we have always translated both *pallavi* and *anupallavi* in full, we have usually chosen only some part of these two lines—sometimes in connection with a later phrase—for our refrains. We hope this will suggest something of the expressive force of the *pallavi* and, in some cases at least, its syntactic linkage with the stanzas, while eliminating lengthy repetition. The headings provide simple contexts for the poems. We have attempted to avoid heavy annotation in the translations, preferring to let the poems speak for themselves. Where a note seemed necessary, we have signaled its existence by placing an asterisk in the text. The source for each poem, as well as its opening phrase in Telugu and the *rāga* in which it is sung, appear beneath the translation.

Editions Used as Base Texts

P. T. Jagannātha Rāvu, ed., *Śṛṅgāra saṅkīrtanalu (annamācārya viracitamulu)*, vol. 18 of *Śrītāḷḷapākavāri geyaracanalu*. Tirupati: Tirumala Tirupati Devasthānam Press, 1964.

Gauripĕddi Rāmasubbaśarma, ed., *Śṛṅgāra saṅkīrtanalu (annamācārya viracitamulu)*, vol. 12 of *Tāḷḷapāka padasāhityamu*. Tirupati: Tirumala Tirupati Devasthānam Press, 1976. (Cited as GR.)

Vissā Appārāvu, ed., *Kṣetrayya padamulu*. 2d ed. Rajahmundry: Saraswati Power Press, 1963. (Unless otherwise noted, all the Kṣetrayya texts are taken from this edition.)

Mañcāḷa Jagannātha Rāvu, ed., *Kṣetrayya padamulu*. Hyderabad: Andhra Pradesh Saṅgīta Nāṭaka Akāḍamī, 1978.

Giḍugu Veṅkaṭa Sītāpati, ed., *Kṣetraya padamulu*. Madras: Kubera Printers Ltd., 1952. (Cited as GVS.)

Śrīnivāsacakravarti, ed., *Kṣetrayya padālu*. Vijayavada: Jayanti Pablikeṣansu, 1966.

Veṭūri Prabhākara Śāstri, ed., *Cāṭupadyamaṇimañjari*. Hyderabad: Veṭūri Prabhākara Śāstri Memorial Trust, 1988 [1913].

Nedunūri Gaṅgādharam, ed., *Sāraṅgapāṇi padamulu*. Rajahmundry: Saraswati Power Press, 1963.

Introduction

On Erotic Devotion

From its formative period in the seventh to ninth centuries onward, South Indian devotional poetry was permeated by erotic themes and images. In the Tamil poems of the Śaiva Nāyaṉmār and the Vaiṣṇava Āḻvārs, god appears frequently as a lover, in roles inherited from the more ancient Tamil love poetry of the so-called *saṅgam* period (the first centuries A.D.). Poems of this sort are generally placed, alongside their classical *saṅgam* models, in the category of *akam*, the "inner" poetry of emotion, especially the varied emotions of love in its changing aspects. Such *akam* poems—addressed ultimately to the god, Śiva or Viṣṇu, and contextualized by a devotional framework, usually that of worship in the god's temple—are early South Indian examples of the literary linkage between mystical devotion and erotic discourse so prevalent in the world's major religions.

A historical continuum stretches from these Tamil poets of devotion all the way to Kṣetrayya and Sāraṅgapāṇi, a millenium later. The *padam* poets clearly draw on the vast cultural reserves of Tamil *bhakti*, in its institutional as well as its affective and personal forms. Their god, like that of the Tamil poet-devotees, is a deity both embodied in temple images and yet finally transcending these icons, and they sing to him with all the emotional and sensual intensity that so clearly characterizes the inner world of medieval South Indian Hinduism.[1] And yet these Telugu devotees also present us with their own irreducible vision, or series of visions, of the divine, at play with the world, and perhaps the most conspicuous attribute of this refashioned cosmology is its powerful erotic coloring. As we seek to understand the import of the Telugu *padams* translated here, we need to ask: What is distinctive about the erotic imagination activated in these works? How do they relate to the earlier tradition of South Indian *bhakti*, with its conventional erotic components? What changes have taken place in the conceptualization of the deity, his human devotee, and the intimate relationship that binds them? Why this hypertrophy of overt eroticism, and what does it mean to love god in this way?

Let us begin with an example from Nammāḻvār, the central poet among the Tamil worshipers of Viṣṇu, who wrote in the southern Tamil area during the eighth century:

> The whole town fast asleep,
> the whole world pitch dark,
> and the seas utterly still,
> when it's one long extended night,
> if He who sleeps on the snake,
> who once devoured the earth, and kept it in his belly,
> will not come to the rescue,
> who will save my life? (5.2.1)
>
> Deep ocean, earth and sky
> hidden away,
> it's one long monstrous night:
> if my Kaṇṇaṉ too,
> dark as the blue lily,
> will not come,

now who will save my life,
sinner that I am?
O heart, you too are not on my side. (5.2.2)

O heart, you too are not on my side.
The long night with no end
has lengthened into an eon.
My Lord Rāma will not come,
with his protecting bow.
I do not know how it will end—
I with all my potent sins,
born as a woman. (5.2.3)

"Those born as women see much grief,
but I'll not look at it," says the Sun
and he hides himself;
our Dark Lord, with red lips and great eyes,
who once measured this earth,
he too will not come.
Who will quell the unthinkable ills
of my heart? (5.2.4)

This lovesickness stands behind me
and torments my heart.
This eon of a night
faces me and buries my sight.
My lord, the wheel forever firm in his hands,
will not come.
So who will save this long life of mine
that finds no end at all? (5.2.6)

The speaker is a young woman, obviously separated from her lover, who is identified as Kaṇṇaṉ/Kṛṣṇa, the Dark God, Rāma, and others—that is, the various forms of Viṣṇu as known to the Āḻvār devotees. The central "fact" stated in each of the verses—which are taken from a closely knit decade on this theme and in this voice—is that the god-lover refuses to come. The woman is alone at night, in an enveloping black, rainy world; everyone else in the village, including her friends and family, has gone to sleep. She, of course, cannot sleep: her heart is tortured by longing, an unfulfilled love that can be redeemed only by the arrival of the recalcitrant lover. She seems quite certain that this will never happen. Her very life is in danger because of this painful inner state, but there is no one to help her. She blames herself, her "sins," her womanhood—and perhaps, by subtle intimation, the god-lover as well, callously sleeping on his serpent-bed (or, in the final verse of the sequence, "engaged in yoga though he seems to sleep").

All in all, it is a picture of plaintive and frustrated desire. It would be all too easy to allegorize the verses, to see here some version of a soul pining for its possessing deity, translated into the language of *akam* love poetry. Indeed, the medieval Vaiṣṇava commentators go some way in this direction, although their allegoresis is neither as mechanical nor as unimaginative as is sometimes claimed.[2] But scholars such as Friedhelm Hardy and Norman Cutler are surely right to insist on the autonomy of the poetic universe alive in the Āḻvārs' *akam* poems. To reduce this poetic autonomy to metaphysical allegory is to destroy the poems' integrity, and with it most of their suggestive power.[3] So we are left with the basic lineaments of the love situation, so delicately drawn in by the poet, and above all with its emotional reality, as the bedrock on which the poem rests. Using the language of classical Tamil poetics, which certainly helped to shape the poem, we can label the situation as proper to the *mullai* landscape of the forests, with its associated state of patient waiting for the absent lover. The god himself,

Māyoṉ, the Dark One (Kṛṣṇa), is the *mullai* deity, and the ceaseless rain is another conventional marker of this landscape.[4] As always in Tamil poetry, the external world is continuous with, and expressive of, inner experience. Thus, in verse 10:

> Even as I melt continually,
> the wide sky melts into a fine mist
> this night,
> and the world just sleeps through it
> saying not a word, not even once,
> that the Lord who paced the earth
> long ago
> will not come.

The heroine is slowly turning to water, "melting," in the language of Tamil devotion, and although there is pain in this state—the pain of unanswered longing—it is also no doubt a stage in the progressive softening (*urukutal*) of the self that Tamil *bhakti* regards as the ultimate process whereby one achieves connection with the object of one's love.

And things are yet more complex. The blackness of night seems to imitate the role of the god; like the latter, the darkness is enveloping, saturating the world. It is also, again like the deity, cruelly indifferent to the heroine's distress—another form of detachment, like the sleep that has overwhelmed the village (and the god). Internal markers of the *mullai* landscape thus resonate and alternate with one another, reinforcing its emotional essence within the speaker's consciousness. And, again, the basic experience is one of separation (Sanskrit: *viraha*), nearly always a constitutive feature of the *bhakti* relationship between god and human devotee. Other features of this relationship are also evident in the poem. For example, one immediately observes the utter asymmetry built into the relation: the heroine, who in some sense speaks for the poet, is relatively helpless vis-à-vis her beloved. She can only wait for him and suffer the torment of his absence. He, in contrast, is free to come or not, to show compassion, if he wishes, and save her life—or let her die of love. There is no way for her to reconstitute his presence. The whole universe proclaims to her his remoteness, seemingly both physical and emotional; she is dwarfed by the inherent lack of equality between them. Interestingly, she blames her situation in part on her womanhood. Being a woman puts her precisely in this position of helpless dependence. She is not even in control of her emotional life: she accuses her heart of having turned against her ("you too are not on my side"), as if a part of herself had split away. This sense of a torn and conflicted personality is typical of the Tamil *bhakti* presentation of self. Overruling passion for the unpredictable and usually distant deity has disrupted the harmony and coherence of the devotee's inner being.

Contrast this picture—blocked desire, unending separation, a world turned dark on many levels, the helplessness of womanhood, a shattered self—with one we find in Kṣetrayya:

Woman! He's none other
than Cĕnnuḍu of Pālagiri.
  Haven't you heard?
  He rules the worlds.

When he wanted you, you took his gold—
but couldn't you tell him your address?
  Some lover you are!
  He's hooked on you.

  And he rules the worlds

I found him wandering the alleyways,
  too shy to ask anyone.
I had to bring him home with me.
Would it have been such a crime
  if you or your girls
had waited for him by the door?
You really think it's enough
to get the money in your hand?
Can't you tell who's big, who's small?
  Who do you think he is?

And he rules the worlds

This handsome Cĕnnuḍu of Pālagiri,
  this Muvva Gopāla,
has fallen to your lot.
When he said he'd come tomorrow,
  couldn't you consent
  just a little?
Did you really have to say no?
What can I say about you?

And he rules the worlds

The senior courtesan or madam is chiding her younger colleague. God himself has come as a customer to this young woman, but she has treated him rather haughtily—taking his money but refusing even to give him her address. The madam finds him wandering the narrow streets of the courtesan colony, too embarrassed to ask for directions. Although his real nature and power are clear enough—as the refrain tells us (and the young courtesan), this customer rules the worlds—it is the woman who has the upper hand in this transaction, while the deity behaves as an awkward and essentially helpless plaything in her control. He wants her, lusts for her, and yet she easily eludes him. Their relationship, such as it is, is transactional and mercenary, and the advantage wholly hers. If Nammāḻvār showed us an asymmetrical bond between the god and his lover (who speaks for the poet-devotee), here the asymmetry, still very much in evidence, is boldly reversed. Moreover, the emotional tone of the Telugu *padam* is radically different from that of the Tamil decade. The atmosphere of tormenting separation, *viraha*, has dissolved, to be replaced by a playful though still far from harmonious tone. God and woman are involved here in a kind of teasing hide-and-seek, with money as part of the stakes, and the woman is an active, independent partner to the game.

It is not always the woman's voice we hear in Kṣetrayya; on rare occasions, the male deity-lover is the speaker. But the image of the woman—the human partner to the transaction—is on the whole quite consistent. Usually, though again not always, she is a courtesan, practiced in the arts of love, which she freely describes in graphic, if formulaic, terms. She tends to be worldly, educated, articulate, perhaps a little given to sarcasm. In most *padams* she has something to complain about, usually her divine lover's new infatuation with some rival woman. So she may be angry at him—although she is also, at times, all too easily appeased, susceptible to his facile oaths of devotion. Indeed, this type of anger—a lover's pique, never entirely or irrevocably serious—is the real equivalent in these poems to the earlier ideology of *viraha*. The relationship thus retains elements of friction and tension, though they are less intense than in the Tamil *bhakti* corpus. Loving god, like loving another human being, is never a simple matter. One might even argue that the god's persistent betrayals, his constant affairs with other women, are felt to be an integral and necessary part of the love bond (just as quarrels are seen as adding spice and verve to love in both Sanskrit erotic poetry and classical Tamil poems). Indeed, these tiffs and sulkings, so perfectly conventionalized, come close to defining the *padam* genre from the point of view of its contents, which sometimes function in a seemingly incongruous context. Thus, in a dance-drama composed during the rule of Vijayarāghava Nāyaka at Tañjāvūr and describing his marriage to a courtesan, the bride sings a *padam* immediately after the wedding ceremony, in which she naturally complains that her husband is (already?) betraying her: "You are telling lies. Why are you trying to hide the red marks *she* left on your lips?"[5]

We should also note that, despite the angry recriminations, the quarrels, and even the heroine's occasional resolve never to see her capricious lover again, many of the *padams* end in an intimation of sexual union and orgasm. A cycle is completed: initial love, sexually realized, leads to the lover's loss of interest or temporary disappearance and to his affairs with other women. But none of this prevents him from returning to make love to the speaker, however disenchanted she may be, as Kṣetrayya tells us:

I can see all the signs
of what you've been doing
till midnight,
you playboy.
Still you come rushing
through the streets,
sly as a thief,
to untie my blouse.

In general, physical union represents a potential resolution of the tensions expressed in many of the poems. In this respect, too, the *padam* contrasts strongly with the Tamil *bhakti* models.

It should now be clear why the courtesan appears as the major figure in this poetry of love. As an expressive vehicle for the manifold relations between devotee and deity, the courtesan offers rich possibilities. She is bold, unattached, free from the constraints of home and family. In some sense, she represents the possibility of choice and spontaneous affection, in opposition to the largely predetermined, and rather calculated, marital tie. She can also manipulate her customers to no small extent, as the devotee wishes and believes he can manipulate his god. But above all, the courtesan signals a particular kind of knowledge, one that achieved preeminence in the late medieval cultural order in South India. Bodily experience becomes a crucial mode of knowing, especially in this devotional context: the courtesan experiences her divine client by taking him physically into her body. Even Annamayya, who is primarily concerned not with courtesans but with a still idealized series of (nonmercenary) love situations, shows us this fascination with bodily knowledge of the god:

Don't you know my house,
garland in the palace of the Love God,
where flowers cast their fragrance everywhere?

Don't you know the house
hidden by tamarind trees,
in that narrow space marked by the two golden hills?

That's where you lose your senses,
where the Love God hunts without fear.

The woman's "house of love" (*madanagṛha*) is the true point of connection between her and the deity-lover. This notion, which is basic to the entire *padam* tradition, takes us considerably beyond the sensual and emotional openness of earlier South Indian *bhakti*. The Tamil devotee worships his deity in a sensually accessible form and through the active exploration of his emotions; he sees, hears, tastes, smells, and, perhaps above all, touches the god. But for the Telugu *padam* poets, the relation has become fully eroticized, in a manner quite devoid of any facile dualistic division between body and metaphysical or psychological substratum. Put starkly, for these devotees love of god is not *like* a sexual experience—as if eros were but a metaphor for devotion (as so many modern South Indian apologists for Kṣetrayya insist). Rather, it is erotic in its own right, and in as comprehensive and consuming a form as one encounters in any human love.

Still, this conceptualization of the relationship does have a literary history, and here we can speak of a series of transformations that take us from *saṅgam* poetry through the Āḻvārs and Nāyaṉmār to the *padam* poets. As already stated, the ancient tradition of Tamil love poetry, with its rich body of conventions, its dramatis personae, and its set themes, was absorbed into the literature of Tamil *bhakti*. In effect, *bhakti* comes to "frame" poems composed after the prototypes of *akam* love poems. The verses from Nammāḻvār cited above, in which the lovesick heroine laments the absence of her lover who is the god, are good examples of this process:

If my Kaṇṇaṉ too,
dark as the blue lily,
will not come,

now who will save my life,
sinner that I am?

What might look like a simple love poem has become something else—a lyric of devotion, which uses the signs and language of *akam* poetics but which subordinates this usage to its new aim by internal reference to the divine object of worship, replete with mythic and iconic identifying traits.[6] By the time we reach the Telugu *padams*, the process has been taken a step further. The "reframed," *bhakti*-oriented love lyric has now acquired yet another frame, which reeroticizes the poem, turning it into a courtesan's love song that is, nonetheless, still impregnated with devotional elements, by virtue of the prehistory of the genre. This development, however, takes somewhat different forms with each of the major *padam* poets and thus needs to be examined more closely, in context, according to the sequence in which it evolved. Indeed, if we focus more on context than content, our perspective on these poems changes significantly. Although all of them, even those seemingly closest to out-and-out love poems, retain a metaphysical aspect, the exigencies and implications of their social and cultural milieux now come to the fore. In what follows, we briefly trace the evolution of the *padam* in context from Annamayya to Kṣetrayya.

On Contexts

Tāḷḷapāka Annamayya composed a song a day for his deity, Lord Veṅkaṭeśvara of the temple on Tirupati Hill, where the Tamil and Telugu lands meet. According to Annamayya's hagiographer—his own grandson, Tiruveṅgaḷanātha—Annamayya's son Pĕda Tirumalayya had these songs inscribed on copperplates together with his own compositions. Considering the total number of songs—Tiruveṅgaḷanātha speaks of some thirty-two thousand[7]—this was a very expensive enterprise indeed, which reflects the status of the poet's family as servants of this most wealthy of the South Indian temple gods. The copperplates were housed in a separate treasure room within the Veṅkaṭeśvara temple at Tirupati; inscriptions suggest that the treasure room was itself an object of worship. Annamayya's songs were probably sung by courtesans who led the processions and danced before the deity in the temple.

The copperplates divide Annamayya's songs into two categories: the metaphysical and the erotic. It is conceivable that Annamayya's career had two corresponding phases, but it is more likely that this classification resulted from a later act of ordering the corpus. In any case, the two categories are reminiscent of Nammāḻvār's poems. Indeed, Annamayya is believed to have been born under the same astrological star as Nammāḻvār and is sometimes regarded as a reincarnation of the Tamil poet. Our first concern, then, is with the manner in which Annamayya uses the language and imagery of eroticism to express his type of devotion.

The courtly tradition in both Sanskrit and Telugu subsumed sexual themes under the category of *śṛṅgārarasa*, the aesthetic experience of desire. Many long erotic poems were composed on mythological subjects, with gods as the protagonists, as well as on more secular themes, with human beings as the heroes. Still, it was considered unsuitable to depict the lovemaking of a god and a goddess, even for devotional purposes; such depictions were thought to block the highest aesthetic experience. (Hence the controversy in Sanskrit aesthetic texts over whether *bhakti* is an aesthetic experience, a *rasa*, or not.) Some even insist that such descriptions constitute a blemish because the god and the goddess are father and mother of the universe; explicit reference to their lovemaking is thus offensive.

But for Annamayya no such barriers exist. He describes how Padmāvatī, Lord Veṅkaṭeśvara's consort, sleeps after making love to her husband:

> Mother, who speaks so sweetly,
> has gone to sleep:
> she has made love to her husband
> with all her feminine skills
>
> and is now sleeping
> long into the day,
> her hair scattered on her face.[8]

Annamayya has songs describing the lovemaking of the goddess, Alamelumaṅga/Padmāvatī, in all conceivable roles and situations. Nor is Annamayya content with love between god and his consort. He goes on to describe the lovemaking of other women with Veṅkaṭeśvara, these women representing every erotic type described in the manuals of love (*kāmaśāstra*).

For Annamayya, love/devotion is an exploration of the ideal experience of the divine. Most often, he assumes the persona of the woman who is in love with the god—either the consort herself or another woman. Unlike later *padam* writers, Annamayya does not describe a courtesan/customer relationship between the devotee and the god. No money changes hands, and the woman does not manipulate the customer to get the best deal. In Annamayya it is always an ideal love relationship, which ultimately achieves harmony. God here is always male, and he is usually in control. He has the upper hand, even when he adopts a subservient posture to please his woman. The woman might complain, get angry, and fight with him, but in the end they make love and the god wins.

When we come to Kṣetrayya, however, the situation is transformed. For one thing, Kṣetrayya composed during the period of Vijayarāghava Nāyaka (1633–1673), the Telugu king who ruled Tañjāvūr and the Kāveri delta. This period witnessed a significant shift, leading to the identification of the king with the deity.[9] Earlier, the god was treated as a king; now the king has become god. For the *bhakti* poets of Andhra, however, especially of Annamayya's period, the king was only too human, at most sharing an aspect of divinity, in the strict Brahminical *dharmaśāstra* tradition. These poets did not recognize him as their true sovereign since for them the real king was the god in the temple. But during the Nāyaka period in South India (roughly the mid-sixteenth to mid-eighteenth centuries), the distinction between the king in his palace and the god in the temple blurs and even disappears. Kṣetrayya could thus address his songs to the king and at the same time invoke the god.

Furthermore, this was also the time when cash began to play a more powerful role in interpersonal transactions. A new elite was emerging, one composed not of landed peasants, as in Vijayanagara times, but of soldier-traders, who cut across traditional social boundaries. These people combined two qualities usually considered incompatible in the Brahminical worldview—martial valor and concern for profit, the quality of a *kṣatriya* (warrior) and the quality of a *vaiśya* (trader). Earlier, when god was king or when the king shared only an aspect of the divine, kingship was ascriptive. To be recognized as a king, one had either to be born in a particular caste as a legitimate heir or to fabricate some such pedigree. Now, in the more fluid social universe of Nāyaka times, ascriptive qualities like birth became less important than acquired qualities like wealth. If a king is god, and if anyone who has money is a king, anyone who has money is also god. For Kṣetrayya, therefore, who sings of kings as gods, the shift to customer as god was not farfetched. Courtesans, who earlier were associated with temples, were now linked to kings—any "king," that is, who had money. The devotional mode, however, did not change. The new god, who was not much more than a wealthy customer, was addressed as Muvva Gopāla, as Kṛṣṇa is known in the local temple.

The shift did not happen overnight. Even in Kṣetrayya we still encounter songs in which the divine aspects are more dominant than those of the human customer. But there are songs unmistakably addressed to the latter. Although the devotional meanings still linger, one sometimes suspects that they are simply part of the idiom, often not much more than a habit. The direction is clear and pronounced when we reach Sāraṅgapāṇi, where money is almost the only thing of value. Here any customer is the god, known as Veṇugopāla (again after the local name of Kṛṣṇa).

We have a slightly earlier precedent for this shift in Rudrakavi's *Janārdanāṣṭakamu*, a composition of eight stanzas that are also sung, though not to elaborate music like the *padams* (nor are they danced to). The theme of this sixteenth-century poem is familiar: the poet assumes the persona of a woman who is in love with the god Janārdana (Kṛṣṇa); she complains that her divine lover is seeing another woman. These songs are very much like Annamayya's, except for one major difference. Here the woman threatens the god, although in the end she is still taken by her cunning lover.

Rudrakavi anticipates Kṣetrayya's attitudes; he represents a transition.

Annamayya's songs (and probably also Rudrakavi's) were sung in the temple. There is, however, no evidence that Kṣetrayya's songs were sung in temple rituals. Kṣetrayya's songs survived among courtesans and in the repertoire of the male Brahmin dancers of the Kūcipūḍi tradition who played female roles. That Kṣetrayya traveled to many places to visit courts and temples is clear from the many specific vocatives in his songs (including one even to the Muslim Padshah of Golconda). As we have already mentioned, temples and palaces were associated with courtesan colonies, and it is quite likely that Kṣetrayya was composing songs for these courtesans to sing—to a deity, king, or customer, the three categories having been, in any case, conflated into one.

We should also note that in these songs the courtesan and the god-customer acquire individual identities. Telugu scholarly tradition later attempted to reduce them to character types, based on conventional Sanskrit texts on erotics and poetics, but such classifications miss the special quality of Kṣetrayya's poems and personae. For instance, women's roles in drama, dance, and poetry were classified into fixed types according to the woman's age, body type, and sexual availability. For example, a heroine is *svīyā*, "one's own wife," *anyā*, "another man's wife," or *sāmānyā*, "common property," like a courtesan. Depending on her experience, she is *mugdhā*, "an innocent," *prauḍhā*, "the bold one," or *madhyā*, "the in-between." Heroines are also classified into eight types according to their attitudes toward their lovers. Permutations and combinations of these and other categories yield a staggering number of different types of heroines. An anonymous late-eighteenth-century Telugu work, the *Śṛṅgārarasamañjari*, attempts to apply such a scheme to Kṣetrayya's songs and even expands the classifications further. Kṣetrayya's depictions are, however, much too individuated to fit any such prefabricated typology.

The attempt to justify these songs by invoking academic (*śāstric*) categories is a characteristic response to perceived needs. First, there was a wish to make Kṣetrayya's work acceptable to scholars—to legitimize his status as a poet in a way that would allow his courtesan songs to be read as poems of *śṛṅgārarasa*, the refined "taste" or "essence" of sexual love, thus giving them a place with the works of the great poets of Sanskrit and courtly Telugu. Second, there was a concomitant desire to dilute the realistic sexuality of the courtesans and to read into these texts elevated meanings of spiritual love. These are two sides of a single process, which requires some further explication if we are to understand the evolution of current attitudes toward Kṣetrayya and his "biography."

Around the turn of the century, with the advent of Victorian moralistic attitudes in public life, sexuality and eroticism in Hindu culture and literature came to be seen as a problem. In the late nineteenth and early twentieth centuries social reformers in Andhra opposed the institution of courtesans per se. Kandukūri Vīreśaliṅgam (1848–1919) started the antinautch movement, which advocated that respectable men should not visit courtesans. Until this time it had been considered prestigious for a man from an upper-caste family to maintain a courtesan. Important men in society prided themselves on their association with courtesan dance groups, which were named after them. People in high positions, such as district magistrates and police commissioners, sponsored courtesan singing groups (*meḷams*); anyone who had business with the officer was expected to attend such performances and give a suitable gift (*ŏsagulu*) to the courtesans, a percentage of which went to the sponsoring officer. As can be imagined, this practice led to corruption in high places. The antinautch movement addressed itself to these social ills with puritanical zeal. But the movement had a negative effect on dance and music. The courtesan had traditionally been the center of song and dance in South India. Housewives were normally prohibited from appearing in public, and certainly from singing or dancing before men. By contrast, the courtesan enjoyed a freedom usually reserved for the men; not only did she not suffer from many of the restrictions imposed on women but she was given the same honor shown to poets in a royal court. Names of great courtesans such as Mācaladevi are known in literature dating from the Kākatīya period.[10] Some, such as the learned Raṅgājamma, were prominent poets in the Nāyaka courts.

But all this was possible only to a woman born in a courtesan caste. By the nineteenth century women born in other castes, for whom marriage was prescribed, were not free to cultivate any of the skills courtesans practiced. Any effort on the part of the family woman even to try to look beautiful or display womanly skills was severely censured. Thus, looking into a mirror at night or wearing too many flowers on certain occasions would bring down the wrath of the elders and accusations that the woman was behaving no better than a courtesan. No insult could be worse: in family households a courtesan was regarded as the most despicable thing a woman could become. By this time, then, the world of women was clearly divided into two opposed parts, that of the courtesan and that of the family woman, and neither of the two wished to be mistaken for the other. Chastity, modesty, innocence, dependency, the responsibility to bear male children to continue the line, and the bringing of prosperity to the family by proper ritual behavior—these were the roles and values assigned to the housewife. These very qualities would be considered defects in a courtesan, whose virtues were beauty, boldness in sex and its cultivation, and a talent for dancing and singing in public. A courtesan could be independent, own property, earn and handle her own money; cunning and coquetry were part of her repertoire. She had no responsibility to bear children, but if she did have a child, a female was preferred to a male. Indeed, a male child in a courtesan's household was both a practical problem and an embarrassment.

Given that these two worlds were so clearly divided, a movement to abolish all courtesans endangered a valuable part of the culture—all that related to song and dance. Granted, in the twentieth century attempts were made to interest young women from respectable families in dance and music so that they could perform in public. Prestigious institutions like Kalakshetra in Madras presented the courtesan dances in a cleaned-up form, renamed the genre Bharata Nāṭyam, and provided it with an antiquity and respectability aimed at making it acceptable to educated, upper-middle-class family women. Still, it was not easy to get these women to sing Kṣetrayya's songs, with all their uninhibited eroticism. Doubts and hesitations persisted. Thus, E. Krishna Iyer writes in his English introduction to G. V. Sītāpati's 1952 edition of Kṣetrayya's *padams*: "Is it proper or safe to encourage present day family girls to go in for Kṣetraya padas and are they likely to handle them with understanding of their true devotional spirit? At any rate can a pada like '*Oka Sarike*' ["if you are so tired after making love just once"] be ever touched by our girls?"[11] Apologetics mix with a palpable fear of the explicit eroticism of these poems, Krishna Iyer arguing that the people of Kṣetrayya's time had a strength of mind we no longer possess.

The trend was now to reinterpret sexual references and representations in Hindu religious texts, ritual, art, and literature by assigning exalted spiritual meanings to them. Even so, many valuable religious and literary texts were proscribed as obscene, while others were published with dots replacing objectionable verses, sometimes spanning whole pages.[12] In an effort to protect traditional texts from disappearing altogether, certain scholars and patrons of art produced limited unexpurgated editions exclusively for scholarly distribution. For works like Kṣetrayya's there was yet no reliable printed edition; the songs were preserved in palm-leaf or paper manuscripts. Scholars like Vissā Appārāvu and patrons like the Mahārājā of Piṭhāpuram (who had long family associations with courtesans) attempted to collect and publish these texts, the Mahārājā, for example, sponsoring G. V. Sītāpati's volume of Kṣetrayya's songs. The effort was laudable and did save the literature from utter extinction. But in order to save the songs the new patrons and scholars "spiritualized" them, arguing that these were by no means erotic courtesan songs. The apparent eroticism was only an allegory for the union of *jīva* and *īśvara*, the yearning human soul and god.

According to hagiographic legends recorded at this stage, Kṣetrayya was above all a devotee. Subbarāma Dīkṣitulu, author of the *Saṅgīta sampradāya pradarśini* (1904), tells a story about "Kṣetrajña," as he calls him in a conspicuously Sanskritized form. This Kṣetrajña, while still a child, was taught a *gopāla mantra* by a great yogi. The boy spent many days uttering the *mantra* in the temple, and eventually the god Gopāla—deity and patron of the erotic—appeared before him and blessed him. Kṣetrajña immediately broke into song. He traveled to the courts of Tañjāvūr, Madurai, and Golconda, composed songs in praise of the kings there, and was honored in turn by those kings.[13] In another story, reported by the scholar Rāḷḷapalli Anantakṛṣṇa Śarma, Kṣetrayya, a singer and poet who had earned the patronage of kings for his songs about them, returned one day to his native village, Muvva, where he fell in love with a courtesan at the local temple of Muvva Gopāla. The courtesan objected that he sang only about kings, never about the god of Muvva, with whom *she* was in love. So, in order to please her, Kṣetrayya sat in meditation for a long time until the god appeared to him and blessed him. From then on, in an ecstasy of divine love, Kṣetrayya went from temple to temple, singing to Muvva Gopāla. That was why he was called Kṣetrayya, one who knows the *kṣetras* or holy places.

Vissā Appārāvu reports that a similar story is told by the villagers of Mŏvva, supposedly Kṣetrayya's place of birth. According to this story, Kṣetrayya's real name was Varadayya. He was an illiterate cowherd who often whiled away his time sitting in the local Gopāla temple. Once he fell in love with a shepherdess (or, in another version, a courtesan) who rejected him because he was an unlettered lout. Varadayya then sat, adamant, inside the temple until the god appeared before him and gave him the gift of song and poetry. Varadayya became a devotee of the god, and his love for the woman was transformed into a spiritual quest in which she, too, took part. The two of them are said to have roamed the countryside, singing together.[14]

This type of story is obviously intended to "reframe," and thereby deeroticize, Kṣetrayya's poetry. Modern Telugu films about Kṣetrayya have also followed this line. Another, perhaps older, type of legend, however, celebrates Kṣetrayya's role as a court poet. Vijayarāghava Nāyaka, the king of Tañjāvūr, is said to have honored Kṣetrayya and given him a high position at court. At this, the other poets grew jealous and complained that it was inappropriate for the king, who was a great scholar himself, to elevate Kṣetrayya to this level. When Kṣetrayya learned of this opposition, he left the last two lines of a song (the *padam* known as *vadaraka po pove*) unfinished, telling the king that he should have it completed by his other poets while Kṣetrayya was away for three months on a pilgrimage.[15] The poets struggled for three months but were unable to complete the poem. When Kṣetrayya returned, the humiliated poets fell at his feet and begged forgiveness for talking ill of him. Kṣetrayya then finished the song. This kind of legend, typically told about court poets such as Kālidāsa, tries to assimilate Kṣetrayya to the category of court poet, whereas the legends retold by Vissā Appārāvu and Rāḷḷapalli Anantakṛṣṇa Śarma attempt to make him into a temple poet.[16] In both cases, though, we observe a similar drive to obscure or explain away the underlying eroticism of the *padam* corpus.

On Reading a Padam

Employing but a small number of themes and voices (the courtesan, the god/customer, a senior courtesan who may even be the madam of the house, and sometimes a married woman who has taken a lover), Kṣetrayya creates a lively variety of poems with unusual details. In one, a married woman who finds herself pregnant berates her lover, demanding that he "go find a root or something" to terminate the pregnancy. In another, a senior courtesan, talking to a younger one who is discontented with her lover, says, somewhat testily, "When your Muvva Gopāla joins you in bed, if you, my lovely, get ticklish, why complain to me?" We have chosen here only one of the poems for detailed comment—and bear in mind that, in other poems, similar devices may carry very different nuances. Even though these poems belong to the tradition of "light" music (as opposed to the classical tradition, though they do find their way into classical repertoires) and some even sound like American pop songs of the "he-done-me-wrong" variety, every one of the poems in this volume would repay the kind of attention we suggest in what follows, however lighthearted, simple, or even pornographic they may appear at first sight. And indeed they are pornographic in the etymological sense of the term: they are songs for and about courtesans (Greek *pornē*, "prostitute").

Here is poem 175 from the Kṣetrayya collection:[17]

A Woman to Her Lover

How soon it's morning already!
There's something new in my heart,
Muvva Gopāla.

Have we talked even a little while
to undo the pain of our separation till now?
You call me in your passion, "Woman, come to me,"
and while your mouth is still on mine,

it's morning already!

Caught in the grip of the Love God,
angry with him, we find release drinking
at each other's lips.

You say, "My girl, your body is tender as a leaf,"
and before you can loosen your tight embrace,

it's morning already!

Listening to my moans as you touch certain spots,
the pet parrot mimics me, and O how we laugh in bed!

You say, "Come close, my girl,"
and make love to me like a wild man, Muvva Gopāla,
and as I get ready to move on top,

it's morning already!

As mentioned earlier, every *padam* begins with an opening stanza, which provides the refrain. This is divided in the original into two parts called *pallavi* and *anupallavi*, refrain and subrefrain. The refrain is repeated at the end of each *caraṇam* or stanza, as the translation suggests, although we have chosen to abridge the refrain to a phrase.

Characteristic of the refrain is the way it brings closure to each stanza yet returns the listener to the opening lines. The refrain completes the sentence, the syntax of the stanza; it also satisfies the expectation of the listener each time it occurs. Thus, with each succeeding stanza there is a progression and at the end of each a regression, a return that nonetheless gives the repeated phrase a new context, a new meaning. In this poem, the stanzas together also move toward a completion of the sexual act, with the lovers asking for more. When the poem is sung or danced to, the *pallavi* line is played with, reached differently each time and variously enacted, suggesting different moods in song and different stances and narrative scenes in a dance performance. In this sense, only the words of the refrain are the same with each repetition: the more it remains the same, the more it changes.

Yet each time the refrain occurs, it laments the lack of completion. *"It's morning already!"* bemoans the frustration of unsated desire. In the original Telugu, all the verbs of the stanza are nonfinite, whereas the verb in the refrain is finite and thus completes the sentence. In terms of meaning, however, the refrain insists on the lack of any satisfying climax and closure. This self-contradictory structure—the form at odds with the meaning—seems to suggest the insatiability of sexual satisfaction. Desire always wants more; the appetite grows on what it feeds on.

This piece—like all Kṣetrayya's poems, even the ones that depict lovers' quarrels and infidelities—ends in union: "and [you] make love to me like a wild man, Muvva Gopāla." Still, the next line, which begins a new sexual move, ends in dissatisfaction, as the speaker blames that intrusive, ever-recurring morning. These features—the context of dance and song, and the poem's very form, which recapitulates desire from arousal to climax and maybe a return to another beginning—give such songs a light-winged quality of celebration and a very physical playfulness. Likewise, the diction of the *padam* tends to the colloquial and the familiar. For example, the language of the poems consists mostly of pure Dravidian words, with very few Sanskritized forms, and the poet often uses the intimate vocative *ra*, which—so a popular oral verse tells us—is appropriate to the speech of young people, to the battlefield, to poetry, and to situations of lovemaking.[18] In general, the sounds reinforce the meanings, often subliminally. For instance, in the second stanza the lines have four second-syllable rhymes: *iddara*, *kŏddigā*, *niddara*, and *muddu*. The soft dental double consonants

(*-dd-*) tend to remind a Telugu speaker of touching, pressing, tightening, embracing, and other such kinesthetic sensations. This particular series also constitutes an internal progression that culminates in *muddu*, a common word for "tender" or "sweet." The poem is thus building toward this moment of tenderness, before the refrain cuts it off with the dawn. Similarly, the last stanza has second-syllable rhymes on liquids—*kaḷala, ciluka, kaliki, kalasi*—which suggest gliding and quick movements. Language-bound as they are, such phonesthemes are impossible to render in another tongue; they are, like so much else in poetry, a translator's despair.

Conclusion

If we compare the *padam* just analyzed to the Nammāḻvār poem with which this introduction began, we can sense the distinct evolution of the *padam* tradition away from its roots in Tamil devotionalism. Here there is no sense that the speaker is in the wrong; she is not waiting eternally for her lover's arrival; there is no landscape of sky and cloud and dark night waiting with her, symbolic of the god's engulfing nature. Nor is the god himself invoked with all his insignia (wheel, mace, lotus feet), nor are we reminded of his many cosmic avatars and acts, against which the speaker's little drama of unrequited love is played out. *Viraha*, separation—a dominant mood in Nammāḻvār and other *bhakti* poets—is here located in the past and thus relegated to the early part of the poem ("Have we talked even a little while to undo the pain of our separation till now?"). If the tradition of love poetry and all its signifiers are enlisted to speak of the human yearning for the divine, here the signifiers of *bhakti* poetry are only fleetingly alluded to, often by no more than the local name of the god, Muvva Gopāla.

To repeat: the original context of the Kṣetrayya *padams* was the courtesan's bedroom, where she entertained a customer identified as a god. No amount of apologetic spiritualizing, no hypertrophied classification in terms of the Sanskrit courtly types, should be allowed to distort the sensibility that gave rise to these poems—even, or especially, if this sensibility has largely died away in contemporary South India. At the same time, we should not make the mistake of underestimating the vitality of the devotional impulse at work in the *padams*. These are still poems embodying an experience of the divine. The *bhakti* idiom is never truly lost through the long process of reframing. One indication of its survival is the existence in the *padams* of strong intertextual resonances, as themes and phrases proper to South Indian devotionalism and familiar from its basic texts are assimilated to the *padam*'s erotic context. Thus Kṣetrayya's heroine complains that she has wasted much of her life in ways remote from her real goal, sexual union with her lover:

When will I get married to the famous Mannāru Raṅga?
A daughter's life in a lord's family,
I wouldn't wish it on my enemies.

Some days pass as your parents do your thinking for you.
Some days pass brooding and waiting for the moment.
Some days pass pondering caste rules.
Meanwhile the bloom of youth is gone
like the fragrance of a flower, like a trick of fate.

I wouldn't wish it on my enemies

The literature of *bhakti* is full of such laments. In Tamil we have Cuntaramūrttināyaṉār (9th century), who often reproaches himself in similar terms:

So much time has been lost! . . .
I have wasted so much time being stubborn.
I don't think of you,
don't keep you in my mind.[19]

Or, in a manner verbally very close to Kṣetrayya's formula:

Those days that I leave you
are the days consciousness fails,
when life leaves the body
and one is carried away
on a high funeral bier.[20]

The precise formula—"some days (*kŏnnāḷḷu*) pass"—occurs elsewhere in Telugu, for example in the *Veṇugopālaśatakamu*, sometimes attributed to Sāraṅgapāṇi (though it was more probably written by a later poet at the Kārveṭinagaram court, Polipĕddi Veṅkaṭarāyakavi):

Some days passed not knowing the difference
  between grief and happiness.
Some days passed in youthful longing for other men's wives,
  without knowing it was a sin.
Some days passed begging kings to fill my stomach,
  as I suffered in poverty.
Time has passed like this ever since I was born,
  swimming in the terrible ocean of life in this world.
O Veṇugopāla, show me compassion in whatever way you
  like,
  just don't take account of my past.[21]

Echoes such as these help establish the *padam*'s peculiar cultural resonance as a devotional genre building upon, but also transforming, powerful literary precedents.

Let us try to sum up and reformulate the distinctive features of this form. Like much of the earlier *bhakti* poetry, the *padam* generally prefers the female voice. Some *padams* present us with the persona of a married woman addressing her lover, in a mode of erotic violation. Here, marriage and the husband function as the necessary backdrop to the excitement of real passion, as in many of the poems of Kṛṣṇa-*bhakti* from Bengal, although in the *padams* the woman largely retains the initiative.[22] But, from Kṣetrayya on, the female voice is most often that of the courtesan, a symbol of open, intensely sensual, but also mercenary and potentially manipulative sexuality. We thus achieve an image of autonomous, even brazen, womanhood, a far cry from the rather helpless female victim of the absent god in Tamil *bhakti*. In other respects, too, the differences are impressive. The torments of *viraha* have given way to less severe tensions relating to the lover's playboy nature, his betrayal of one courtesan with another, his irrepressible mischief and erotic games. Desire is far less likely to be blocked forever, and many of the poems culminate in orgasm, often openly mentioned. This, then, is more a poetry of union than of separation. In contrast to the torn female personality of Tamil *bhakti*, the courtesan in these poems is remarkably self-possessed. Indeed, the balance of power has dramatically shifted, so that it is the god who frequently loses himself in this woman, while she is capable of toying with her lover, feigning anger, or mercilessly teasing him. She may also, of course, be truly abandoned, left languishing in ways reminiscent of earlier models, but more often she embodies a mode of experiencing the divine that is characterized by emotional freedom, concrete physical satisfaction, and active control. It is the courtesan, after all, who has only to name her price. Undoubtedly the most trenchant expression of this perspective is the anonymous *padam* addressed to Lord Kōṅkaṇeśvara:

I'm not like the others.
You may enter my house,
but only if you have the money.

If you don't have as much as I ask,
a little less would do.
But I'll not accept very little,
Lord Kōṅkaṇeśvara.

To step across the threshold
of my main door,
it'll cost you a hundred in gold.
For two hundred you can see my bedroom,
my bed of silk,
and climb into it.

Only if you have the money

To sit by my side
and to put your hand
boldly insidc my sari:
that will cost ten thousand.

And seventy thousand
will get you a touch
of my full round breasts.

Only if you have the money

Three crores to bring
your mouth close to mine,
touch my lips and kiss.
To hug me tight,

to touch my place of love,
and get to total union,
listen well,
you must bathe me
in a shower of gold.

But only if you have the money

What could be clearer than this escalating scale of prices? The god can decide for himself what he wants—or rather, can afford. One is reminded, somewhat ironically, of the list of rituals, each with its set price, performed for pilgrims at South Indian temples. There, however, it is the devotee who pays the fee, while the god, addressed in the act of worship, is the ultimate beneficiary of the gift. An even more powerful inversion—and an indication of just how far the *padam* tradition has traveled away from earlier *bhakti* models—is expressed in an image painted by the Vīraśaiva poet Basavaṇṇa (12th century), with reference to rituals of a different sort:

I drink the water we wash your feet with,
I eat the food of worship,
and I say it's yours, everything,
goods, life, honour:
he's really the whore who takes every last bit
of her night's wages,

and will take no words
for payment,

he, my lord of the meeting rivers![23]

The Songs

Annamayya

A Woman to Her Lover

Don't you know my house,
garland in the palace of the Love God,
where flowers cast their fragrance everywhere?

Don't you know the house
hidden by tamarind trees,
in that narrow space marked by the two golden hills?

That's where you lose your senses,
where the Love God hunts without fear.

Don't you know my house?

Don't you know the house,
the Love God's marketplace of passions,
the dusk where the dark clears and yet is not clear?

Don't you know the house
where you live in your own heart?
That's where all affections hold court.

Don't you know my house?

Don't you know the house
where the garden of daturas make you go mad with love?
You should know: you're the lord of Veṅkaṭa hill.

Its gates are signed by the Love God,
and you should know that's where
you heap all your wealth.

Don't you know my house?

Annamayya 262, GR
"maruninagari daṇḍa"
rāga: śrī

The Other Woman to Veṅkaṭeśa

Why blame me that I'm jealous?
When she's with you,
shouldn't I be embarrassed?

When you and she talk in private,
shouldn't I stay outside the gate?

When you signal each other with your hands,
shouldn't I hide and look away?

When she's with you

When you and she look at each other's faces
with me around, shouldn't I hide my face
in my hands?

When you two are covered in a shawl,
isn't it right for me to go play dice?

When she's with you

When your Alamelu* is here in town for you,
what's left for me to do but bow my head
to the two of you?

O Veṅkaṭeśa, the two of you have ruled me.
Isn't it a pleasure to serve you both?

When she's with you

Annamayya, copperplate 485:448
"ĕnta kucciturālanṭā"
rāga: mukhāri

Her Friends Tease the Woman in Love

These marks of black musk
on her lips
red as buds,
what are they
but letters of love
sent by our lady to her lord?

Her eyes the eyes of a *cakora* bird,
why are they red in the corners?

Think it over, my friends:
what is it but the blood
    still staining the long glances
    that pierced her beloved
after she drew them from his body
back to her eyes?

What are they but letters of love?

How is it that this woman's breasts
show so bright through her sari?

Can't you guess, my friends?
What are they but rays from the crescents
    left by the nails of her lover
    pressing her in his passion,

rays now luminous as the moonlight
of a summer night?

What are they but letters of love?

What are these graces, these pearls
raining down your cheeks?

Can't you imagine, friends?
What could they be but the beads of sweat
    left on her lotus-face
    by the Lord of the Hills
when he pressed hard,
frantic in love?

What are they but letters of love?

Annamayya 82, GR
"emŏkŏ ciguruṭadharamuna"
rāga: nādanāmakriya

A Woman Talking to Herself

Better keep one's distance
than love and part—
especially if one can't manage
seizures of passion.

Make love, get close, ask for more—
but it's hard to separate and burn.
Gaze and open your eyes to desire,
then you can't bear to shut it out.

Better keep one's distance

The first tight embrace is easy,
but later you can never let go.
Begin your love talk—
once hooked, you can never forget.

Better keep one's distance

Twining and joining, you can laugh;
soon you can't hide the love in your heart.
Once the lord of the Lady on the Flower
has made love to you,
you can no longer say
it was this much and that much.

Better keep one's distance

Annamayya, copperplate 484:440
"tagili pāyuṭa kaṇṭe"
rāga: āhiri

A Woman to Her Lover

O you lover of whores:
I know your ways,
I can see them all.
Why do you need a mirror to see
the jewel on your wrist?

Some woman has tried to hug you hard
with her hand covered with bracelets.
I can still see the print of their curves
on your shoulder. Why tell me lies?
I know your tricks.

You lover of whores, why do you need a mirror?

Some woman has comfortably slept
on your chest and the sapphires
of her necklace have left a print
on your skin. Why contest it over and over?
O you love expert, I can't be harsh.

You lover of whores, why do you need a mirror?

Some woman has made love to you,
Lord of Veṅkaṭa hill,
plundered your body's perfumes.

Soon after, you come into my arms.
How can I blame you? My weariness is gone.

You lover of whores, why do you need a mirror?

Annamayya 84, GR
"lañjakāḍav'auduvurā"
rāga: āhiri

Rudrakavi

Eight on Janārdana of Kandukūru

1 You've come, haven't you,
showing off your beauty,
your shining gold-embroidered shawl
slipping from your shoulder,
body casting moonbeams on your lotus-feet,
with your enchanting form surpassing all,
rider of the Garuḍa bird,
crusher of demons,

O Janārdana of Kandukūru.

2 Three days ago,
in spite of my oaths,
you didn't show.
Let it go.
The day before yesterday
I kept calling you,
but you didn't hear.
You sneaked away.
Yesterday, even as I was looking,
you walked away,
dressed to kill.
Just you wait!
you great crusher of demons,

you Janārdana of Kandukūru.

3 You and she,
you spent last night
in the alcove together.
I heard everything you did
from a woman I know.
I didn't just hear it,
I saw you on the street
with my own eyes,
you crusher of demons,

you Janārdana of Kandukūru.

4 Who was that shy girl
who left those little red marks
on your lips?
Who was she
with such big breasts
who has fallen for you?
Who pressed your cheeks
and left finger marks
with nails sharp as knives,
you crusher of demons,

you Janārdana of Kandukūru?

5 I know all your secrets.
Don't make false promises.
Don't come to me, over and over,
with those drowsy, clouded eyes.
Keep your clumsy hands

off my body.
Don't work yourself up
over me, you stubborn
crusher of demons,

you Janārdana of Kandukūru!

6 You were my constant support,
but that was once.
Why burn and get angry now?
Go back to where you came from.
Stop! I can't bear your words.
You're a big scoundrel,
O crusher of demons,

Janārdana of Kandukūru.

7 All my anger is gone.
When did you come close to me?
When did you give me
those jewels with nine gems?
Loving me, and making me love you,
being one with me,
you cover me with praise.
When did you do all this,
O crusher of demons,

Janārdana of Kandukūru?

8 When you fill my two eyes,
it's a flowering of jasmine.
I watch the skies, the clouds
color everything.
Why does moonlight
shine in my eyes?
I've seen it all,
you crusher of demons,

*Janārdana of Kandukūru.**

Kṣetrayya

The Madam to a Courtesan

Woman! He's none other
than Cĕnnuḍu of Pālagiri.
    Haven't you heard?
    He rules the worlds.

When he wanted you, you took his gold—
but couldn't you tell him your address?
    Some lover you are!
    He's hooked on you.

And he rules the worlds

I found him wandering the alleyways,
    too shy to ask anyone.
I had to bring him home with me.
Would it have been such a crime
    if you or your girls
had waited for him by the door?
You really think it's enough
to get the money in your hand?
Can't you tell who's big, who's small?
    Who do you think he is?

And he rules the worlds

This handsome Cĕnnuḍu of Pālagiri,
    this Muvva Gopāla,
has falled to your lot.

When he said he'd come tomorrow,
    couldn't you consent
    just a little?
Did you really have to say no?
What can I say about you?

And he rules the worlds

Kṣetrayya 176
"cĕllabo pālagiri cĕnnuḍe vīḍu kŏmmā"
rāga: śaṅkarābharaṇamu

A Woman to Her Lover

"Your body is my body,"
you used to say,
and it has come true,
Muvva Gopāla.

Though I was with you
all these days,
I wasn't sure.

Some woman has scratched
nail marks on your chest,
but I'm the one who feels the hurt.

You go sleepless all night,
but it's my eyes
that turn red.

"Your body is my body," you used to say

Ever since you fell for that woman,
it's my mind
that's in distress.

When I look at those charming love bites
she has left on your lips,
it's my lip that shakes.

"Your body is my body," you used to say

Maybe you made love
to another woman,
for, O lord who rules me,
my desire is sated.

Forgive me, Gopāla,
but when you come back here,
I'm the one who feels small
with shame.

"Your body is my body," you used to say

Kṣetrayya, GVS 1:2
"nī menu nā men'anucunu"
rāga: yadukula kāmbhoji

A Man Speaks of His Love

What can I do to cool my passion?
Who will bring her,
that gem of a woman,
back to me?

I was able to draw your face,
bright as a lotus,
but could I paint in
its fragrance?

I have drawn your lips,
glowing with desire,
but I couldn't put in
their honey.

Who will bring her?

I knew how to draw
your lovely eyes,
but not the trembling glance;

painted the soft lines
of the throat
I know so well,
but could not fill it
with birdlike tones.

Who will bring her?

I even painted
the lovemaking,
bodies coiled
in the Snake Position,

but I couldn't paint you
as you cried, all alive,
"Come, come to me again,
Muvva Gopāla!"

Who will bring her?

Kṣetrayya 126
"emi seyudu"
rāga: kāmbhoji

A Courtesan to a Young Customer

You are handsome, aren't you,
Ādivarāha,*
and quite skilled at it, too.

Stop these foolish games.
You think there are no other men
in these parts?
Asking for me on credit,
Ādivarāha?
I told you even then
I won't stand for your lies.

Handsome, aren't you?

Prince of playboys you may be,
but is it fair
to ask me to forget the money?
I earned it, after all,
by spending time with you.
Stop this trickery at once.
Put up the gold you owe me
and then you can talk,
Ādivarāha.

Handsome, aren't you?

Young man:
why are you trying to talk big,
as if you were Muvva Gopāla?

You can make love like nobody else,
but just don't make promises
you can't keep.
Pay up,
it's wrong to break your word.

Handsome, aren't you?

Kṣetrayya 1
"andagāḍav'auduvu lerā"
rāga: śaṅkarābharaṇamu

A Young Woman to a Friend

Those women, they deceived me.
They told me he was a woman,
and now my heart is troubled
by what he did.

First I thought
she was my aunt and uncle's daughter,
so I bow to her, and she blesses me:
"You'll get married soon,
don't be bashful. *I* will bring you
the man of your heart."

"Those firm little breasts of yours
will soon
grow round and full," she says.

And she fondles them
and scratches them
with the edge of her nail.

"Come eat with me," she says,
as she holds me close
and feeds me as at a wedding.

Those women, they told me he was a woman!

Then she announces:
"My husband is not in town.

Come home with me."
So I go and sleep in her bed.

After a while she says,
"I'm bored. Let's play
a kissing game, shall we?
Too bad we're both women."

Then, as she sees me falling asleep,
off my guard,
she tries some
strange things on me.

Those women, they told me he was a woman!

She says, "I can't sleep.
Let's do what men do."
Thinking "she" was a woman,
I get on top of him.

Then he doesn't let go:
he holds me so tight
he loses himself in me.
Wicked as ever, he declares:

"I am your Muvva Gopāla!"
And he touches me expertly
and makes love to me.

Those women, they told me he was a woman!

Kṣetrayya 264
"mosabuccir'amma magavāni yāḍad'aṇṭa"
rāga: sāveri

A Courtesan to Her Lover

Who was that woman sleeping
in the space between you and me?
Muvva Gopāla, you sly one:
I heard her bangles jingle.

As I would kiss you now and then,
I took her lips into mine,
the lips of that woman fragrant as camphor.
You must have kissed her long.

But when I tasted them,
they were insipid
as the chewed-out fiber
of sugarcane.

Who was that woman?

Thinking it was you, I reached out for a hug.
Those big breasts collided with mine.
That seemed a little strange,
but I didn't make a fuss
lest I hurt you, lord,
and I turned aside.

Who was that woman?

You made love to me first,
and then was it her turn?
Does she come here every day?

Muvva Gopāla,
you who fathered the god of desire,
you can't be trusted.
I know your tricks now
and the truth of your heart.

Who was that woman?

Kṣetrayya 61
"iddari sanduna"
rāga: kalyāṇi

A Courtesan to Her Friend

It's so late.
He's not coming,
no way.
No use worrying about him.

Just because you've the misfortune
to be my friend,
you needn't wait up till dawn.
You can throw away
the sandal and the musk
and go to sleep.
Who knows where
he is spending the night,
and with what woman?
The whole village is fast asleep.

It's so late

Listen: every bird
has gone home to his mate.
It's rare we get what we desire.
Still, what was my special sin?

It's so late

All excited,
I made the bedroom ready,
waiting for my man.
What's the point now

of these ornaments,
all these flowers?
Who will see this beauty?
He's not to be trusted,
this Muvva Gopāla,
who has ruled in my bed.

It's so late

Kṣetrayya 37
"inta prodd'āyĕ"
rāga: pantuvarāḷi

The Courtesan Speaks to Her Lover

I'm seeing you at last.
It's been four or five months,
Muvva Gopāla!

Last night in my dream
you took shape before my eyes.
I got up with a start,
looked for you,
didn't find you.
The top of my sari
was soaked with tears.
I turned to water,
gave in to sorrow.
I asked myself
if you might not
be thinking of me, too.

I'm seeing you at last,
the answer to my prayers

Ever since we parted,
there's been no betel for me,
no food,
no fun,
no sleep.
I'm like a lone woman
in a forest
after sunset,

soaked through by the rain
in the heavy dark,
unable to find a way.

I'm seeing you at last,
the answer to my prayers

My parents blame me,
my girlfriends mock.
This may sound strange,
but I can tell you:
ever since we first made love,
my world
has become you.
I have no mind
other than yours.

I'm seeing you at last,
the answer to my prayers

Kṣetrayya 213
"ninnu jūḍa galigĕne"
rāga: punnāgavarāḷi

A Courtesan to Her Lover

Why are you so taken? Is she really
more beautiful than all these women?
You can't stop looking at her for a moment.
Why don't you speak your mind?

Does she come to you
flowing with affection
to gather you up in her embrace?
Does she roll you betel leaves,
praise you as the lover
most suited to her love?

Does her passion overwhelm?
I'd love to hear the details
over and over
of what you do
when your minds are one.
Tell me now.

Why are you so taken?

Does she let you drink at her lips,
make you beg for one more and one more?
Bring you flowers,
tell you how right you are
for her beauty?

Does she really give you her heart?
Tell me the name of that woman

who prayed to the god of desire
to have you for a husband.
You don't have to be shy.

Why are you so taken?

Does she dance with pleasure,
pluck the strings and sing
seductive songs?
Invent new ways of making love
and plead with you then
not to stop,
even as she celebrates your skill?
What's left?
Why tell lies, Muvva Gopāla,
when clearly she's the one you crave
while all the time you're making love
to me?

Why are you so taken?

Kṣetrayya 39
"inta moham'emi rā"
rāga: śaṅkarābharaṇamu

A Woman to Her Friend

Friend, I didn't say a word.
It would be a shame
if others were to hear.

He came with a glisten of mascara
still on his lips.
When I said it hurt me,
he made a scene.

When my friends asked me
what had happened,
I laughed it off,
covered it up.

I didn't say a word

He wasn't afraid to come home
with the red lac from *her* feet
on his forehead.
Still, he had the nerve
to ask for a hug.

I was furious
but, hiding it,
I protested gently.
I said it wasn't right.
He raised his voice and,

fearing where it might lead,
I gave in.

As in the saying
about the thorn and the banana leaf,
it's always the leaf that gets torn.

I didn't say a word

Friend, he came here
with her betel juice
staining his neck,
yet asked me for a kiss.
It seemed improper
to hurt a man
who had come to me.

But when he made love to me
as well as ever,
I felt obliged, and

I didn't say a word

Kṣetrayya 229
"nor'ĕttan'aitin'ammā"
rāga: kāmbhoji

A Courtesan to a Messenger

Why does he send an embassy, standing right in front of me?
Ask him to come in, that Muvva Gopāla:
he once fathered the Love God.

There he is, all dressed up;
as the women watch,
he displays his charms.
He stands at the main door and complains,
he curses me every day.
I don't know how long he has stood there.

But why send an embassy?

Yesterday he seems to have come all the way here
at midnight and then he turns back—
some maid tells him this is no time to visit:
what are we, princesses?

But why send an embassy?

What, hasn't he come and gone as he pleases?
Hasn't he ever joined me in bed?
Now do I have to go all the way and give him a reception?
Maybe my Muvva Gopāla is just testing my heart.

But why send an embassy?

Kṣetrayya 269
"ramm anave"
rāga: kedāra

A Woman to Her Reluctant Lover

Because I'm a good woman, I forgave you this time.
Would any other woman have let you off?

You follow me around like a servant,
you say humble things,
yet when I ask you to come home, you don't.
Why do you hurt me like this?

Now I've got you all alone.
If I hold you prisoner in this house,
who is there to release you?

Because I'm a good woman

You hold my hands, you say nice things.
But when I ask you to get into bed,
you say, "I've taken a vow," and do nothing.

Now I've caught you.
If I tie you down to my bed,
who is there to release you?

Because I'm a good woman

Only for a bet in a game you enter my bedroom.
When I call you, "My handsome,

my Muvva Gopāla!" why this indifference, dear parrot
in the hand of the Love God?

If I choose to make love to you now,
who is there to stop me?

Because I'm a good woman

Kṣetrayya 228
"nenu mañcidāna"
rāga: pantuvarāḷi

An Older Woman to a Younger

Why complain to me? What are you, a little girl?
Was it a crime to bring you two together? Well, well.

When you two play at love as husband and wife,
if he says something against you, you answer back!

Why complain to me?

When he pulls your sari in his passion,
tell him it's not fair!

Why complain to me?

When your Muvva Gopāla joins you in bed,
if you, my lovely, get ticklish,

Why complain to me?

Kṣetrayya 204
"nann'anevā"
rāga: mukhāri

A Woman to Her Friend

When will I get married to the famous Mannāru Raṅga?
A daughter's life in a lord's family,
I wouldn't wish it on my enemies.

Some days pass as your parents do your thinking for you.
Some days pass brooding and waiting for the moment.
Some days pass pondering caste rules.
Meanwhile the bloom of youth is gone
like the fragrance of a flower, like a trick of fate.

I wouldn't wish it on my enemies

Some days pass without any pleasure from your husband.
Some days pass in mere courtesies.
Some days pass in the pride that we are palace women,
looking for quality.
It's a pity all this high passion is like moonlight in a forest.

I wouldn't wish it on my enemies

Some days pass shilly-shallying, knowing and not knowing.
Some days pass ignorant of the ways of experience.
Some days pass listening to friends' stories of lovemaking.
Alas, womanhood itself has become my enemy,
and I'm tired.

I wouldn't wish it on my enemies

Kṣestrayya, GVS 5:17
"perubaḍa"
rāga: nāṭakurañji

A Woman to Her Messenger

Has he forgotten me or what?
Go ask him. He knows.

He knows how I went to fetch water.
He knows where he stood at the shore.
He knows when he rattled the chain on the door.
He knows how he asked me, hungrily, to show him my breasts.

Go ask him, he knows

He knows how he begged me.
He knows how he seductively tossed his kerchief at me.
He knows how he shook his head and laughed.
He knows how he couldn't bear it any more.

Go ask him, he knows

He knows where he left tooth marks on my lips.
He knows how he said, folding me in his arms, he is Muvva Gopāla.
He knows the sheets we were wrapped in.
And he knows how he made room
and played the Love God with me.

Go ask him, he knows

Kṣetrayya 251
"maracināḍ'aṭa"
rāga: gauḷipantu

A Married Woman to Her Lover

Let me go now to the man
    who put the marriage chain* round my neck,
for how long can a married woman stay
    in her mother's house, Muvva Gopāla?

I can be back in a month for my sister's wedding.
Meanwhile, friend, don't forget our friendship.

This is the only way for family women
    and it's laid down by the gods.
If your kindness lasts,
    this body belongs to you.

Let me go for now

Couldn't you come and visit me once when the fair is on?
And give me the ring as a mark of love.

You say you can't bear to be away:
    that goes for both of us.
When again and again I beg leave to go,
    don't hold me back by talking.

Let me go for now

We have done it once. Why don't you let me leave?
Muvva Gopāla, is it fair to pester me like this?

If people around hear about us,
    won't it be disastrous?
There's no other way, what can I do?
    God is not pleased with us.

Let me go for now

Kṣetrayya, GVS 1:18
"boṭṭugaṭṭina"
rāga: bhairavi

A Woman to Her Friend

Friend, tell me, who is more wicked, he or I?
Explain it. Now we'll know who's what.

When we are on the bed of gold,
　　playing at love talk,
he calls me Kamalākshi,
　　the other woman's name:
I am so mad, I hit him as hard as I can with my braid.

　　　Now tell me, who is more wicked?

When lustily I jump on top
　　and pound his chest
with my pointed nipples, he says,
　　"That girl Kanakāṅgi is very good at this."
I slap him hard with all five fingers.

　　　Now tell me, who is more wicked?

After making love, as always,
　　I fondle his feet, soft as a young leaf,
when the other woman's
　　love potion goes to his head,
he talks in his sleep about her,
　　lying right next to me:
so I sink my teeth into his lips.

　　　Now tell me, who is more wicked?

Kṣetrayya 104
"ĕvarivalla duḍuku"
rāga: suraṭa

A Courtesan to Her Messenger

Today is a good day. Let him come like a prince.

Maybe that woman has been watching Muvva Gopāla.
So what? Isn't this body of mine his property?
In this business I'm in,
    is it right to rant and rave?

Let him come like a prince

Should I leave him just because he is kind?
Tell him then I won't fault him if he mentions her name.
When he comes, I won't treat him any different.
    Isn't this place his house?

Let him come like a prince

Besides, I'm just as pretty as that pretty thing.
Who took him to task? Not I. Why get a bad name for nothing?
When Muvva Gopāla himself makes love to her and likes it,
    who am I to say it isn't proper?

Let him come like a prince

Kṣetrayya, GVS 1:28
"mañci dinamu neḍe"
rāga: ānandabhairavi

A Wife to a Friend

Don't tell me what he did in some other country.
What has it got to do with me? For god's sake, stop it.
What are you saying: that he went to her house, fell for her,
  gave her money and begged her?

More likely, she saw his beauty, wanted him,
fell all over him, begged him, melted him with her music.
After all, he's a man. He couldn't contain himself, that's all.

Don't tell me what he did

All decked in jewelry like a wild cassia in bloom,
a temptress on a mission from the Love God,
she must have stood there and said,
"Hey, handsome! It's not good for you to stay alone.
Come over and sleep in my house."

Don't tell me what he did

That Muvva Gopāla, Lord of Madhura, from the day
he made love to me he hasn't known anyone else.
Nor is he up to any tricks, he is a dignified man.
He must have been angry that I wasn't anywhere near.

Don't tell me what he did

Kṣetrayya 233
"paradeśamuna"
rāga: mohana

A Girlfriend to the Woman

Woman: that Varada* loves you so.
I'm here because I couldn't watch him suffer.

He puts his hand on his cheek,
smiles his little smile,
and says to himself,
"Oh I knew it:
she'll never come back.
I can't forget
the love we had before.
To live without making love
to that lovely girl—
is that called living?"

That Varada, he loves you so

He is quiet for a while,
and then he sighs:
"Where did I go wrong?
I can't bear
to be apart from you
even for a little while.
My mouth cannot speak," he says,
and buries his head in his hands.
If I ask, he only says,
"What help can you be?"

That Varada, he loves you so

That Varada, that Muvva Gopāla,
he babbles on and on.
"The miracle
that happened then,
will it happen again?"
He thinks, and sighs,
and sighs again,
and says, "This is what fate has done.
This dreadful thing
called love—
I wouldn't wish it on my enemies."

That Varada, he loves you so

Kṣetrayya 43
"intiro varaduniki"
rāga: dhanyāsi

A Woman to Her Friend

What can he do worse than this?
And what's left?
Out of sheer spite,
he stays in that woman's house.

When I go hungrily to embrace him,
he says, "Stay away!"
When innocently I say,
"Give me the honey of your lips,"
he says, "That's pollution."
When I say, without thinking,
"Give me a bit of that betel in your mouth,"
he yells at me and says, "No!"
Such indifference
in front of my peers
is too much!

What can he do worse?

When I'm close,
if I offer to roll betel for him,
he says, "Not my taste."
If I say, "Let me look at your face
from this far,"
he says, "No, don't."
When I go to massage his feet,
he says, "It's too late. Go away."

He says, "I've forgotten
all my love for you."

What can he do worse?

Even to people
in the street he says,
"My love for her has turned."
He vows never to speak
nicely to me again.
Arguing, he says,
"I want nothing to do with you"—
and gives me the betel*—
this same Muvva Gopāla
who once so lustily
made love to me.

Whan can he do worse than this?

Kṣetrayya 33
"intakaṇṭe dā nann'emi cesīni"
rāga: pantuvarāḷi

A Courtesan to Her Lover

Pour gold as high as I stand, I still won't sleep with you.
Why be stubborn, Muvva Gopāla? Why all these tricks?

You set women afloat on your words,
break into their secret places,
deceive them with affectionate lies,
excite them in love play,
get together the whole crowd one day,
and then you steal away like a spinach thief.

Pour gold as high as I stand

You coax women's affections,
make them amorous and faint,
do things you shouldn't be doing,
confuse them, lie in bed with them,
and then you leave without a sound,
shaking your dust all over them.

Pour gold as high as I stand

You opportunist,
you excite them from moment to moment,
make mouths water,
show them love to make them surrender,
drown them in a sea of passion,

and by the time the morning star appears—
you get up and vanish.

Pour gold as high as I stand

Kṣetrayya 216
"niluvuna niliveḍu"
rāga: kalyāṇi

A Woman to Her Friend

Go ask him:
is it for nothing I get angry?
Don't be naive.

Go ask him and make him swear
to tell the truth

When my maid runs into him
when he is on his way
to that woman's house,
who gets scared
and offers her the bribe,
is it him or is it me?

I'm not imagining things.
Who is it that said
before all the neighborhood women,
"I can't live without seeing that woman,"
is it him or is it me?

Go ask him and make him swear

Standing on her doorstep
as if he had no fears,
who sees me in the street

and hides behind the door?
Is it him or is it me?

When he comes home tired
and I give him porridge with sugar,
who is it that says,
"The taste isn't half as good as her lips,"
is it him or is it me?

Go ask him and make him swear

Languishing, who draws
her picture on a slate,
holds it in his palm
and stares at it,
is it him or is it me?

When, in making love,
I embrace Muvva Gopāla,
who sighs and sighs
for that other woman,
is it him or is it me?

Go ask him and make him swear
to tell the truth

Kṣetrayya 9
"aḍugar'ammā"
rāga: mukhāri

A Married Woman Speaks to Her Lover

I can't stay too long.
I have to get home.
There's no time for all the fun.
Don't get me in trouble,
my clever man.

I left my husband's embrace
to come here
just because you called.
You want to leave your nail marks
on my breasts—
I'm no prostitute!

I have no quarrel with you.
Satisfy your need
and send me away.
Listen, lover:
it's not good for your health
to lose too much sleep.
Why argue with me?

Can't stay too long

You're biting my lips too hard.
How can I hide the marks?
Because sugarcane is sweet,
you want to pull it up,
root and all.

It's hard to bear.
Just because I'm so taken with you,
you trap me in your net of magic,
you clever man.

Can't stay too long

You've made love to me often enough
for today.
Let go for now, Muvva Gopāla,
my lord.
Is it right to be stubborn now?
Is there a limit to greed?
The more you make love,
the more you want it.
This body of mine is your property.
I'll come whenever you want me.
Be good to me,
my clever man.

Can't stay too long

Kṣetrayya 55
"iccoṭanu cāla prŏdd'uṇḍa cĕlladu"
rāga: kāmbhoji

A Woman to Her Girlfriends

What can I do about this?
What can I say?
This stupid heart of mine
has lost all shame.

When I hear from the girls
that he has gone to her house,
I promise myself
I'll swear an oath and say:
Don't ever come here.
But the moment I see his face,
my desire doubles.
Where does it go,
my fury, a tigress
with new cubs?

This stupid heart

I hear he has sent gifts to her door
and I decide I'll never see his face.
And you know what happens?
He comes to me, holds me,
and I don't even remember my rage.

This stupid heart

I hear he was seen in her house
and I decide: from now on,
I'll make his life miserable.
Then that Muvva Gopāla,
he comes happily
and makes love to me,
and I forget all my vows.

This stupid heart

Kṣetrayya 47
"induku nen'emi setune"
rāga: bilahari

A Courtesan to Her Girlfriend

Fate that brought us together
so soon has put us apart.
No point in thinking:
that's what I get
for all my worship.

Did we spend even six months
happily in one place?
When I was hurting, passionate for love,
were our minds really one?

I only suffered the scandal,
but did we ever spend an hour
touching thigh to thigh?
Did we ever have a day whispering
each other's names?

Fate has put us apart

Did my lord and I, any day,
play properly
at love?
Did we ever press
lip to red lip,
tasting the sweetness?

Fate has put us apart

Did we ever lie twined,
till we were done,

in each other's arms?
In bed, did we ever play
even for fun
at husband and wife?

Fate has put us apart

Did we ever sing, in pleasure,
even one measly song
about Muvva Gopāla?
Did we ever talk sweetly
about nothing in particular,
lying on flowers?
Did we ever stay up all night
long after sundown?

Fate has put us apart

Time that brought us close
has left me burning:
fate that brought us together
so soon has put us apart.

Kṣetrayya 41
"intalone allavāni nannu gūrci"
rāga: yadukula kāmbhoji

A Married Woman to Her Lover

My old husband is better than you, and that's the truth.
You promise sweet things in private
and only now you show your face!

Where can I hide my desire,
to whom shall I give it now?
Enough, enough, go away.
Enough of this adventure at this ungodly hour!

My old husband is better than you!

Like a parrot waiting
for the fruit of the silk-cotton tree
I fell for your looks
and came to you.

My old husband is better than you!

Fighting off sleep all night
waiting for you, it was like pouring
into water what was meant for a fire.
It's late. I've got to go home, Muvva Gopāla.

My old husband is better than you!

Kṣetrayya 217
"nīkannā nā mŏguḍe melu"
rāga: navaroju

A Courtesan to the Messenger

Don't go on chattering, just go away.
Why should he come here?
Tell him not to come.

It all happened so long ago,
in a different age,
another life.
Who is he to me, anyway?

Think of the long nights I spent
waiting for him, minute after minute,
saying to myself, "He'll come today,
he'll come tomorrow!"—

the hot sighs,
lips dry with longing,
nights aflame with moonlight.
What more is there to say?

Just go away!

I wore myself out watching the road.
Counting the moons, I grieved.
Holding back a love I could not hold,

listening to the screeching
of peacocks and parrots,
I passed the months of spring.
Let's have no more empty words.

Just go away!

I even asked the birds for omens
if Muvva Gopāla was coming.
I grew weak, watching my girlfriends
join their husbands for love.

O god, do I ever have to see
his face again
with this body of mine?
Once was enough!

Just go away!

Kṣetrayya 283
"vadaraka po pove"
rāga: kāmbhoji

A Courtesan to Her Friend

Let him go as he pleases.
Friend, let my lord Muvva Gopāla go as he pleases.

I hear
he begged his girlfriend,
bowed to her, folding both his hands,
complained of this and that to her about me,
and he promised her things, behind the temple.

Let my lord be well, wherever he is, that's enough.

Let him go as he pleases

I hear he said
he would be struck by evil if he even looked
in my direction;
he fingered his mustache and bragged to her.
I hear
he said my name, broke a reed
and threw it away.*

A thousand qualities at every step, who can straighten him out?

Let him go as he pleases

I hear he said
he first made love to me just because he was tricked;

he swore to god never to touch me again;
in an assembly he said I'm a brazen woman.

Yet if love has taken root in his heart, he'll be kind one day.

Let him go as he pleases

Kṣetrayya 181
"tana cittamu"
rāga: mukhāri

A Senior Courtesan to a Younger One

Are you done with your anger?
Have you finally talked, my dear,
to one another,
you and your Muvva Gopāla,
and stopped being angry
at last?

Have your hearts cooled off
and found a little peace?
Tell me the truth:
is all that grieving
over for today?
Could you finally have
one good day?
He over there,
you here,
with these endless sighs in between!

Are you done with your anger?

Have you looked
at each other's faces,
taken sweet kisses
from your lips,
pressed body against body?
Why treat one another
like a hunter and his prey?

Are you done with your anger?

Today, at least,
have you shared a single bed
and praised, I hope,
each other's skills in love?
You've finally come together,
haven't you,
you and your Muvva Gopāla,
confessing over and over
that you listened to slander
like fools.

Are you done with your anger?

Kṣetrayya 25
"aluka dīrĕnā"
rāga: sāraṅga

A Courtesan to a Messenger

You want to know, my graceful friend,
how skilled he has become
at making love?
Just go bring that Muvva Gopāla to me.

All I know is that he came here,
smiling that smile of his,
and took me by the hand,
but I don't even know that he took off the sari
from my breast.

I know he combed down my long hair
and covered it with flowers,
but I know nothing of those violent
red lips
pressed on mine.

Just go bring that Muvva Gopāla to me

I know he leaned toward my ear
to tell me secrets,
but I couldn't hear
his words.

I know he kissed my neck
with passion,
but I don't know
of any fingernails
clawing at my cheeks.

Just go bring that Muvva Gopāla to me

I know he embraced me,
my lover, Muvva Gopāla,
but I know nothing
about the crush
of our two bodies.

You know, my friend
with the body of a flower,
that I don't really know
he untied the knot of my sari
and did, inside me,
whatever he has done.

Just go bring that Muvva Gopāla to me

Kṣetrayya 17
"ammamma vīḍ'ĕnta"
rāga: māruva

A Married Woman to Her Lover

Go find a root or something.
I have no girlfriends here I can trust.

When I swore at you, you didn't listen.
You said all my curses were blessings.
You grabbed me, you bastard,
and had me by force.
I've now missed my period,
and my husband is not in town.

Go find a root or something

I have set myself up for blame.
What's the use of blaming you?
I've even lost my taste for food.
What can I do now?
Go to the midwives and get me a drug
before the women begin to talk.

Go find a root or something

As if he fell from the ceiling,
my husband is suddenly home.
He made love to me last night.
Now I fear no scandal.
All my wishes, Muvva Gopāla,

have reached their end,
so, in your image,
I'll bear you a son.

Go find a root or something

Kṣetrayya 296
"vētaki terā poyi"
rāga: begaḍa

A Woman to Her Lover

If your mind is like mine,
my prayers will be answered.
As if sugarcane should begin to bear fruit,
my pleasures would be doubled many times

if your mind is like mine

If aimlessly I doodle with my fingernail,
it's your shape that appears.
The moment I wake from sleep,
it seems you're close to me.
You know such is my love, Varada.
To whom can I say

your mind is like mine?

If I turn
as I go upstairs
and see my shadow,
I feel you're coming with me.

When I sing with the *tambura* drone,*
it feels like you are singing along.
The very sound of what I say
sounds like your reply.
There's nothing like my love, Varada.
You know that: to whom can I say

your mind is like mine?

I'm always filled with joy,
and the joy is always
of holding you.

Even if I think your name,
O Varada with the goddess,*
it's as if we're making love.
It pleases me
when all my girlfriends
say you're my friend.
You alone
know the secret of my longing.
Whom can I ask

if your mind is like mine?

Kṣetrayya, GVA 3:62
"nā manasuvaṇṭidi"
rāga: kalyāṇi

A Woman to Her Friend

The lord who always slept
with his head on my breasts
is—*ayyayyo!*—now sick of me.

His eyes fixed, unblinking,
on my face,
he would say,
"When dusk falls,
your face, alas,
will be hidden in the dark,"
and than ask me,
in broad daylight,
for a lamp.

Ayyayyo, he's now sick of me

Biting my mouth in love play,
since to talk would be to let go,
my lord would speak only
with his hands.

Ayyayyo, he's now sick of me

Lest in sleep
his embrace should loosen,

he would ask me to tie down
the four corners of our blanket.

Ayyayyo, he's now sick of me

Kṣetrayya 20
"ayyayyo vĕgaṭ'āyĕne"
rāga: nādanāmakriya

A Courtesan to Her Lover

Why have you come here? Go away,
her house is not here on this street.

Muvva Gopāla,
you who lifted the Mandara mountain,*
are you here looking for that woman
with teeth like jasmine buds?

You must have lost your way
in this flooding moonlight,
or else you lost yourself
in that woman, with eyes darting
like fish.

I know I'm not the one
who embraced you
and put your mind at rest.

Go away, her house is not here

I can see all the signs
of what you've been doing
till midnight,
you wicked man.

Still you come rushing
through the streets,
sly as a thief,
hurrying to untie my blouse.

Go away, her house is not here

You're much too drunk with passion
to leave me.
Stop now.
You're making love to me
with twice the fury.
It's morning.
Get up,
before the women come
and see us.

Go away, her house is not here

Kṣetrayya 310
"ind' ĕndu vaccitivi rā"
rāga: suraṭi

A Woman to Her Friend

If the betel girl* goes with him,
wouldn't it be a scandal?
My Muvva Gopāla has gone astray.

When I'm not around he worships her
with his eyes.
Like a randy rogue,
he puckers his mouth for a kiss.

When he takes the folded betel from her,
he's thrilled and scratches her hand
with his fingernail.

She backs away and says,
"O no! With me, it's wrong!"
and comes running to me in haste.

Wouldn't it be a scandal!

It seems he says, "People are around.
Close the door and come in."
Again and again, he makes obscene jokes.

When she says, "No, don't come too close,"
he tries to put his hand in her sari.
Because she's a proper woman, she talks back
and comes running to me.

Wouldn't it be a scandal!

It seems he says, "I'm here only for you."
He even gnashes his teeth and threatens her.
He says, "Look, if I don't make love to you,
then call me a betel woman."

And to think
I rushed to make friends
with this Muvva Gopāla!

Wouldn't it be a scandal!

Kṣetrayya 8
"aḍapagattě vāṇivaṇṭid'aite"
rāga: pantuvarāḷi

A *Woman to Her Lover*

How soon it's morning already!
There's something new in my heart,
    Muvva Gopāla.

Have we talked even a little while
to undo the pain of our separation till now?
You call me in your passion, "Woman, come to me,"
and while your mouth is still on mine,

it's morning already!

Caught in the grip of the Love God,
angry with him, we find release drinking
at each other's lips.

You say, "My girl, your body is tender as a leaf,"
and before you can loosen your tight embrace,

it's morning already!

Listening to my moans as you touch certain spots,
the pet parrot mimics me, and O how we laugh in bed!

You say, "Come close, my girl,"
and make love to me like a wild man, Muvva Gopāla,
and as I get ready to move on top,

it's morning already!

Kṣetrayya 175
"cĕllabo yĕnta vegame"
rāga: useni

Śāraṅgapāṇi

The Madam to a Courtesan

He pays you in rupees of lead
knotted to your sari:
couldn't you even check,
you fool?

He makes promises,
then works on you till dawn,
that Muvva Gopāla,
and pays you in rupees of lead.

Like an honest man, he sends you letters,
that cheat who turns you on,
then eats you out of betel leaves,
sticks his tongue out at you,

and pays you in rupees of lead

Holds you tight,
not letting you go,
attacks and wounds
your lips,
touching you in places
you don't let anyone touch,
making you shameless.

Plucks a hair off his body
and throws it at your house,

and pays you in rupees of lead

Makes love to you
and rouses you,
then tucks the pleats
of your sari back in place.

If you fall asleep,
he slaps you awake
and shows you what he's got,

and pays you in rupees of lead

Sāraṅgapāṇi 99
"sīsapu rūkalu"
rāga: saurāṣṭra

A Customer to a Courtesan

Is there any rule
that it must be you?
If I have money,
there's always your sister.

Or if not her, her sister.
No one does it for merit.
Even Rambhā in heaven
demands her fee.*

Where was this love of yours
when I came begging to you then
and fell, infatuated,
at your feet?

Didn't you say you wouldn't talk
unless you got the pendant?
If I scatter rice,
will there be a shortage of crows?

There's always your sister

When I put in your box
a sixty-rupee roll of *nagiri* silk,
didn't you wear it as a frock?
If it rains, will it cure my welts?

There's always your sister

So what if you called to me, "Veṇugopāla!"
craved me,
made love on top of me?
It's even better
than the story of the date-palm seed.

Why would a picotta* stoop so low
except to bring water
from the depths?

There's always your sister

Sāraṅgapāṇi 102
"nīv'enā"
rāga: mohana

The Madam to a Young Courtesan

Grab whatever cash he has,
that Veṇugopāla,
and think nothing of the rest.

As they say about lentils,
don't worry
about the chaff.

Does it matter
to which woman he goes,
or how late he stays there?

Just pass the days
saying yes and no,
till the month is over

and grab the cash

What is it to you
if he runs into debt
or if he has an income?

Quietly, tactfully,
lie in wait
like a cat on a wall

and grab the cash

What if he makes love
to her
and only then to you?

What's there
to be jealous about?
When youth passes,
nothing will go your way,

so grab the cash

Sāraṅgapāṇi 98
"kaligina kāsu"
rāga: saurāṣṭra

A Married Woman's Complaint

If my husband becomes my pimp,
what am I then to him?

Veṇugopāla throws away money,
and says to my husband,
"I'll build you a two-storied house;
look at these ornaments,
this cartload of vessels,"
and adds, "You won't have a worry in the world":

so my husband becomes my pimp

The man says he can't earn any more.
He's fed up with working.
Not even one child is in good shape.
And if I don't agree,
he'll renounce the world.

My husband becomes my pimp.

He says he can't take poverty,
that whoring is no sin,
especially with his permission.
If I don't consent,
he calls me "Ah, Super-Chaste."
He can't wait
to see me sell myself.

My husband becomes my pimp

He says you can't cross
a husband's word,
and cites a thousand
precedents in the texts.
Past sixty, and in his dotage,

my husband becomes my pimp

He says I should sleep
with Veṇugopāla,
dress up like a harlot.
But is life worth more than honor?
Friend, tomorrow he'll find out
for himself.

My husband becomes my pimp

Sāraṅgapāṇi 124
"iṇṭi magaḍu"
rāga: dhanyāsi

A Wife's Complaint

How is this household
going to survive?
Tell me what to do
with all these lewd antics
of lord Veṇugopāla,
scion of the Gokula clan.

Takes no care of his house.
Finds good advice bitter.
Wants special meals.
Hangs out with pimps.

Tell me what to do

Sleeps in whorehouses.
Throws away money on sluts.
Scratches his creditors
for luxuries,
with not a drop of ghee
in our house.

Tell me what to do

But there's no end of dancing songs,
not to speak of the lute.
He bets on cocks at the fights.*

Tell me what to do

I have a single sari to wear and to wash.
Can't even mention a second blouse.
Turmeric has become my gold,
and my ears are bare.

Tell me what to do

And then I have to listen daily
to his affairs with those women.
Even my curses don't stir him.

It's been seven years
since we've been in bed.
Women of my age
are mothers of children.

Tell me what to do

Sāraṅgapāṇi 127
"ī kāpuram'ĕṭl'ākṛti"
rāga: ānandabhairavi

To an Older Woman

All those days he called you,
you were too proud.
Now you're circling
his house.

Are you in love,
after you're past
the age for men?
Don't be coquettish now.
All those days Veṇugopāla called you,
you were too proud.

Now you're circling his house

Hasn't your face
hardened with age?
Pale lips,
wobbling rows of teeth,
body lustreless,
beauty dulled.
But all those days that kind man
fell at your feet and begged,
you were too proud.

Now you're circling his house

Look at you:
half your hair is gray.
You barely look like a woman.

Forty, and nearsighted,
you don't have breath enough to sing.
All those days that handsome man
begged you not to be cross,
you were too proud.

Now you're circling his house

You've cleaned up
your place of love
and made it look new.
You've come alone
at this time of night
on this lonely path.
If Veṇugopāla does you the favor
of sleeping with you,
won't people laugh?

Now you're circling his house

Sāraṅgapāṇi 128
"pilacina nāḍ'ĕlla"
rāga: bilahari

Poem to Lord Kōṅkaṇeśvara

A Courtesan to Her Lover

I'm not like the others.
You may enter my house,
but only if you have the money.

If you don't have as much as I ask,
a little less would do.
But I'll not accept very little,
Lord Kōṅkaṇeśvara.

To step across the threshold
of my main door,
it'll cost you a hundred in gold.
For two hundred you can see my bedroom,
my bed of silk,
and climb into it.

Only if you have the money

To sit by my side
and to put your hand
boldly inside my sari:
that will cost ten thousand.

And seventy thousand
will get you a touch
of my full round breasts.

Only if you have the money

Three crores to bring
your mouth close to mine,
touch my lips and kiss.
To hug me tight,
to touch my place of love,
and get to total union,

listen well,
you must bathe me
in a shower of gold.

*But only if you have the money**

Anonymous
"intaku galigite"
rāga: bilahari

Notes and Index of Refrains

Notes to the Text

Preface

1. See Barbara Stoler Miller, *Love Song of the Dark Lord: Jayadeva's Gītagovinda* (New York: Columbia University Press, 1977), pp. 7–14.

2. Telugu is a Dravidian language spoken by some fifty million people in the present-day state of Andhra Pradesh.

3. Matthew Allen has completed a Ph.D. dissertation at Wesleyan University on the Tamil *padam* tradition: "The Tamil Padam: A Dance-Music Genre of South India" (1992).

4. There is some controversy over the earlier of Tāḷḷapāka's dates, since it can be read in different ways in the relevant copperplate inscription. See Veṭūri Ānandamūrti, *Tāḷḷapākakavula kṛtulu, vividha sāhitīprakriyalu* (Hyderabad: Privately published, 1974), vol. 1, p. 60.

5. Vissā Appārāvu, ed., *Kṣetrayya padamulu*, 2d ed. (Rajahmundry: Saraswati Power Press, 1963), song no. 297.

6. See Velcheru Narayana Rao, David Shulman, and Sanjay Subrahmanyam, *Symbols of Substance: Court and State in Nāyaka Period Tamil Nadu* (Delhi: Oxford University Press, 1992).

7. One of Kṣetrayya's *padams* tells us that the courtesans must be able to write down and read back the *padams* composed by their royal lover. See Vissā Appārāvu, ed., *Kṣetrayya padamulu*, p. 213.

8. See *Śṛṅgārapadamulu*, P. Sītāpati and K. Veṅkaṭeśvara Rāvu, eds., with an introduction by Vaḍlamūḍi Gopālakṛṣṇayya (Hyderabad: Andhra Pradesh Government Oriental Manuscripts Library and Research Institute, 1972).

Introduction

1. On Tamil *bhakti*, see Friedhelm E. Hardy, *Viraha-bhakti: The Early History of Kṛṣṇa Devotion in South India* (Delhi: Oxford University Press, 1983); Norman Cutler, *Songs of Experience: The Poetics of Tamil*

Devotion (Bloomington: Indiana University Press, 1987); Indira Viswanathan Peterson, *Poems to Śiva: The Hymns of the Tamil Saints* (Princeton: Princeton University Press, 1979); and A. K. Ramanujan, *Hymns for the Drowning* (Princeton: Princeton University Press, 1979).

2. On allegoresis in the medieval commentaries, see Cutler, *Songs of Experience*, pp. 93–110; and F. Clooney, "I Created Land and Sea: A Tamil Case of God-Consciousness and Its Śrīvaiṣṇava Interpretation," *Numen* 35, Fasc. 2 (1988): 238–59.

3. Hardy, *Viraha-bhakti*, pp. 318–25, Cutler, *Songs of Experience*, pp. 93–110. See also Ramanujan, *Hymns for the Drowning*, p. 155.

4. See A. K. Ramanujan, *Poems of Love and War* (New York: Columbia University Press, 1985), pp. 236–43, on the conventions of *akam* poetry.

5. *Vijayarāghavakalyāṇamu* of Koneṭi Dīkṣitulu, in Gaṇṭi Jogisomāyaji, ed., *Yakṣagānamulu (Tañjāvūru)*, vol. 2 (Waltair: Andhra University, 1956), p. 187.

6. See Ramanujan, *Hymns for the Drowning*, p. 160.

7. This number is based on the literary evidence given by Tāḷḷapāka Cina Tiruveṅgaḷanātha in his *Annamācāryacaritra*, ed. Veṭūri Prabhākara Śāstri (Tirupati: Tirumala Tirupati Devasthānam Press, 1949), p. 45. The actual number of available songs is much smaller: 14,358 according to Veṭūri Ānandamūrti, *Tāḷḷapākakavula padakavitalu: Bhāṣāprayogaviśeṣālu* (Hyderabad: Privately published, 1976), p. 74.

8. Annamayya, *palukutenĕla talli pavaḷiñcĕnu*: see Veṭūri Prabhākara Śāstri, ed., *Śṛṅgāra saṅkīrtanalu*, vol. 4 (Tirupati: Tirumala Tirupati Devasthānam Press, 1974), song no. 74.

9. For a full discussion of this development, see Velcheru Narayana Rao, David Shulman, and Sanjay Subrahmanyam, *Symbols of Substance: Court and State in Nāyaka Period Tamil Nadu* (Delhi: Oxford University Press, 1992).

10. See the *Krīḍābhirāmamu* of Vallabharāya (15th century?), Baṇḍāru Tammayya, ed. (Madras: Vavilla Ramaswami Sastrulu & Sons, 1953), verse 180.

11. E. Krishna Iyer, introduction to Giḍugu Veṅkaṭa Sītāpati, ed., *Kṣetraya padamulu* (Madras: Kubera Printers Ltd., 1952), p. xix.

12. Even Vissā Appārāvu's generally reliable edition (*Kṣetrayya padamulu*, 2d ed. [Rajahmundry: Saraswati Power Press, 1963]) occasionally

succumbs to this temptation, as, for example, on p. 81. The often highly explicit Nāyaka-period *śṛṅgārakāvyas* proved particularly vulnerable to this type of editing, especially given prevailing Victorian sensibilities. Early editions of Śeṣamu Veṅkaṭapati's *Tārāśaśāṅkavijayamu*, for example, often replace whole sections of text, which describe lovers' union, with asterisks.

13. Subbarāma Dīkṣitulu, *Saṅgīta sampradāya pradarśini*, 2d ed., 2 vols. (Hyderabad: Andhra Pradesh Sangita Nataka Akadami, 1973), 1:9.

14. Vissā Appārāvu, *Kṣetrayya padamulu*, pp. 7–9; Appārāvu includes the version reported by Rāḷḷapalli Anantakṛṣṇa Śarma.

15. For a translation of this *padam*, see pp. 109–10.

16. On these categories, see the afterword to Hank Heifetz and V. Narayana Rao, *For the Lord of the Animals—Poems from the Telugu: The Kāḷahastīśvara Śatakamu of Dhūrjaṭi* (Berkeley: University of California Press, 1988).

17. We give the Telugu original for those who wish to consult it:

ఉసేని - చాపు

చెల్లబో యెంతవేగమే - తెల్లవారెరా!
ఉల్లములో జాలవింతై - యున్నది మువ్వగోపాల /చెల్లబో/

ఇద్దరమీ వరదాక - నెడబాసిన వెతదీర!
కొద్దిగా నింతసేపైన - సుద్దులాడుకొంటిమో?
నిద్దరమైన తమిదీర - నెలత రా రమ్మని నీవు
ముద్దు బెట్టిన నీమోవినా- మోవిపైనున్నదెంతలోనే /చెల్లబో/

చెలువుడ! నీవు నేను - వలరాజు చేజిక్కిన
యలకదీర మోవి తేనె - లానుకొంటి యుంటిమో?
తలరాకుబోణి!రమ్మని - దయతోడ నీవిచ్చినట్టి
వలపుల బిగికౌగిలి - వదలలేదింతలోనే /చెల్లబో/

కళలంటి నేబలికిన - పలకులువిని ముద్దు
చిలుక పలికినందుకింత - సేపు నవ్వకొంటిమో?
కలికిరో!రమ్మని నన్ను - కడువేడ్క మువ్వగోపాల
కలిసి యుపరతినేనై - గమకించేటంతలోనే /చెల్లబో/

18. The verse reads *cinnappuḍu ratikeḷikan' unnappuḍu kavitalona yuddhamulonan vannĕ sumī rākoṭṭuṭa cĕnnugano pūsapāṭi sītārāmā*: see Veṭūri Prabhākara Śastri, ed., *Cāṭupadyamaṇimañjari* (Hyderabad: Veṭūri Prabhākara Śāstri Memorial Trust, 1988 [1913]), verse 526.

19. David Shulman, *Songs of the Harsh Devotee: The Tēvāram of Cuntaramūrttināyaṉār* (Philadelphia: Department of South Asia Regional Studies, University of Pennsylvania, 1990), verses 616 and 617.

20. Ibid., verse 490.

21. *Veṇugopālaśatakamu* (Madras: N. V. Gopal & Co., 1962), verse 33. For an earlier example from the *padam* corpus, see Annamayya's poem *nimiṣam'ĕḍa tĕgaka . . . nidurace kŏnnāḷḷu neramula kŏnnāḷḷu*. We thank Soṇṭhi Śāradāpūrṇa for this reference.

22. See Edward C. Dimock, *The Place of the Hidden Moon: Erotic Mysticism in the Vaiṣṇava-sahajiyā Cult of Bengal*, 2d. ed. (Chicago: University of Chicago Press, 1989), and "Doctrine and Practice among the Vaiṣṇavas of Bengal," in Milton Singer, ed., *Krishna: Myths, Rites, and Attitudes* (Honolulu: East-West Center Press, University of Hawaii, 1966), especially pp. 60–63.

23. A. K. Ramanujan, *Speaking of Śiva* (Baltimore: Penguin Books, 1973), p. 81. Reproduced by permission of Penguin Books Ltd.

Notes to the Songs

47.15. Alamelu: A shortened form of Alemelumaṅga, a name for Veṅkaṭeśvara's consort derived from the Tamil *alar mel maṅkai*, "the lady on a flower." This goddess, assimilated to Lakṣmī, is described as a woman standing on a lotus. Vĕṅkaṭeśa is another name of the god Veṅkaṭeśvara of Tirupati, in Andhra Pradesh.

60.1–9 When you fill my two eyes . . .: The last verse follows the text given in the *Telugu kāvyamāla*, ed. Kāṭūri Veṅkaṭeśvara Rāvu (New Delhi: Sahitya Akademi, 1976), p. 148, rather than that of the *Cāṭupadyamaṇimañjari*, ed. Veṭūri Prabhākara Śāstri, pp. 81–82. For the various versions of this text, see Kandukūri Rudrakavi, *Janārdanāṣṭakamu* (Madras: Ānandamohana Kāvyamāla, 1966).

69.2. Adivarāha: A name of Viṣṇu alluding to his incarnation as a boar (*varāha*).

89.2. The marriage chain: The *maṅgalasūtram*, or *tāli boṭṭu*, which is tied around the bride's neck by the groom at the time of their wedding.

94.1. Varada: A short name, meaning "giver of boons," for Varadarājeśvarasvāmi, a form of Viṣṇu worshiped in the famous temple at Kāñci, in South India.

97.11. Betel: Also called *pan,* a combination of betel leaf, areca nut, and other ingredients, chewed for pleasure. Contracts and ritual events are marked by an exchange of betel, and here "gives me the betel" serves as a kind of "quit notice," signaling that the affair is over.

111.14–16. I hear he said my name . . .: This verse, which does not appear in the Appārāvu edition of the *Kṣetrayya padamulu*, has been taken from the Śrīnivāsacakravarti edition, p. 115.

119.17. When I sing with the *tambura* drone . . .: The text of this stanza follows the version that appears in the *Sāraṅgapāṇi padamulu*, ed. Puripaṇḍā Appalasvāmi (Rajahmundry: Saraswati Power Press, 1963), p. 13.

120.5. O Varada with the goddess: The original has the name of the goddess, Perundevi, another name of Lakṣmī, the wife of the presiding deity in Kāñci, Varadarājeśvarasvāmi, to whom this song is addressed.

123.4. You who lifted the Mandara mountain: According to myth, Kṛṣṇa lifted this mountain to protect cows from a hailstorm brought on by Indra, the king of the gods, who is also the god of rain.

125.1. The betel girl: An *aḍapakattĕ*, a servant girl in the courtesan's house who carries betel in a special box.

133.7–8. Even Rambhā in heaven: Rambhā is the courtesan of Indra, the king of the gods.

134.6. Why would a picotta: A picotta is an old device for raising water from a well that continues to be commonly used in India, especially in farming. It consists primarily of a long horizontal wooden pole with a bucket at one end. We have not been able to trace the reference to the story of the date-palm seed.

139.21. He bets on cocks at the fights: One line from this stanza has been omitted because it is unintelligible.

146.11. We thank Matthew Allen for supplying us with the original of this *padam*, which is cited by Jon B. Higgins in "The Music of Bharata Nāṭyam" (Ph.D. diss., Wesleyan University, 1973), pp. 279–80. Higgins reports that the great dancer Balasaraswati taught him this *padam* in response to his request for a song about a *sāmānya nāyikā* (a courtesan). Balasaraswati noted that she did *not* dance this *padam!*

Index of Refrains

And grab the cash, 135
And he rules the worlds, 63
And pays you in rupees of lead, 131
Are you done with your anger?, 113
Ayyayyo, he's now sick of me, 121
Because I'm a good woman, 84
Better keep one's distance, 51
But why send an embassy?, 83
Can't stay too long, 102
Don't tell me what he did, 93
Don't you know my house?, 45
Fate has put us apart, 106
Go ask him and make him swear to tell the truth, 100
Go ask him, he knows, 88
Go away, her house is not here, 123
Go find a root or something, 117
Handsome, aren't you?, 69
I didn't say a word, 81
If your mind is like mine, 119
I'm seeing you at last, the answer to my prayers, 77
It's morning already!, 127
It's so late, 75
I wouldn't wish it on my enemies, 87
Just go away!, 109
Just go bring that Muvva Gopāla, to me, 115
Let him come like a prince, 92
Let him go as he pleases, 111
Let me go for now, 89
My old husband is better than you!, 108

Now tell me, who is more wicked?, 91
Now you're circling his house, 141
O Janārdana of Kandukūru, 57
Only if you have the money, 145
Pour gold as high as I stand, 98
So my husband becomes my pimp, 137
Tell me what to do, 139
That Varada, he loves you so, 94
There's always your sister, 133
This stupid heart, 104
Those women, they told me he was a woman!, 71
What are they but letters of love?, 49
What can he do worse?, 96
When she's with you, 47
Who was that woman?, 73
Who will bring her?, 67
Why are you so taken?, 79
Why complain to me?, 86
Wouldn't it be a scandal!, 125
You lover of whores, why do you need a mirror?, 52
"Your body is my body," you used to say, 65

Designers: Ina Clausen & Barbara Jellow
Compositor: G&S Typesetters, Inc.
Text: 10/15 Electra
Display: Electra
Calligraphy: Erma Takeda
Printer: Thomson Shore
Binder: Thomson Shore